W9-CFL-535

# Hand Made Baking

# HAND MADE baking

## RECIPES TO WARM THE HEART

KAMRAN SIDDIQI

Library of Congress Cataloging-in-Publication Data:

Siddiqi, Kamran.
Hand made baking : recipes to warm the heart / by Kamran Siddiqi.
pages cm
Includes index.
ISBN 978-1-4521-1230-5
1. Baking. 2. Baked goods. I. Title.

TX763.S447 2014
641.81'5--dc23

2014005141

Manufactured in China

Design by Alice Chau
Photography and styling by Kamran Siddiqi



10 9 8 7 6 5 4 3 2 1

Chronicle Books LLC
680 Second Street
San Francisco, California 94107
www.chroniclebooks.com

*To the timeless romantic sitting alone in the corner of a café, the ravenous cookbookworm, the home baker, the timid cook, and the parent covered in flour and frosting at midnight. This book is for you.*

–KS

# contents

# introduction

Most of us seek congruity, peace, and harmony in our lives, whether we do it through standing shoulder to shoulder in a small kitchen sharing laughs with our loved ones, writing in complete and utter silence, watching reruns of our favorite television shows, or opening the curtains on a summer morning to discover a picturesque day waiting outside the window.

Peace, for me, is the feeling of waking up early on a Saturday morning, ready to take on the day with full energy. It's the background sound of people snoring. It's the feeling of standing barefoot on the cold gray-and-blue Jackson Pollock–esque linoleum floor of a kitchen, wearing oversize basketball shorts and a blue pin-striped shirt that could easily accommodate two. It's the feeling of a cool autumn breeze capering through the kitchen like a Punjabi bhangra dancer. Peace is the reassuring feeling of my arm wrapped around a large mixing bowl filled with chocolate cake batter.

Baking is my peace. It's what I do on nights when I can't sleep. Music is set to play in the background, the oven is turned on, and I open to a page in my baking journal and begin the beautiful dance of late-night baking.

I am a twenty-two-year-old baker and cook brought up on good food in New York City, which brims with restaurants and bakeries on nearly every street corner. Growing up, visits to bakeries were a constant; I was raised on good bagels, unbelievably flaky and buttery croissants, artisanal breads of all kinds, and pastries and cakes made by sweet Russian babushkas and Italian nonnas.

I am the only baker on either side of my huge family; I started baking at the age of five and my love for this form of comfort cooking blossomed from then on. During my formative years, my parents drifted apart and later divorced; my mother, sister, and I picked up from the only place we knew as home, New York City, and moved to the suburbs of New Jersey. The entire act of leaving one's home is a shock; if you've experienced leaving home before, you know how much of an anxiety-inducing experience it can be. Getting used to the sounds of New Jersey and the mix of emotions running through my mind during that time of my life left me sleepless at night, so I'd find myself baking in the kitchen while listening to Norah Jones. Baking, since then, has always been my method of seeking solace and therapy.

Both sides of my family come from very different cultures. My father hails from Pakistan, while his family hails from India and other countries. My mother was born in New York City's Chinatown to a Spanish father and a mother from the Dominican Republic. Because of my very diverse background, I've been encouraged throughout my life to eat and experience different cuisines—many of which are related to my cultures, and some that aren't. Because of this, a great number of relatives who introduced me to these many cuisines influenced the recipes in this book. Neither side of my family expected me to be writing about food in a book; even I didn't expect it. Before I entered college, I planned to become a forensic anthropologist. Then, two weeks before freshman orientation, I decided to pursue writing. Specifically, I wanted a career that involved writing about my biggest passion: food.

This was something I had never before thought about doing, and when I announced my choice, my family thought I'd gone mad. Suddenly I couldn't see myself being a scientist, isolated in a lab, working to solve the arcane. Instead I saw myself writing and sharing good food with others, just as I did on my blog, The Sophisticated Gourmet, putting myself out there to show everyone that rolling up your sleeves and giving any recipe a good try shouldn't be feared, but embraced. If I hadn't been befriended by an amazing community of food lovers when I started The Sophisticated Gourmet during the end of my sophomore year of high school, I'd never have made the decision to dream big. Many of my ambitions of sharing good food and teaching others to embrace old and new tastes are rooted in my blog.

This book is my biggest attempt yet at doing just that on a larger level. It's an attempt to convert fear-filled nonbakers to experts in this ultimate form of comfort-food cooking. It's also an attempt to help you build your confidence in the kitchen, with your love for family, friends, and sharing at the center of all your work.

Baking, to me, is about the clattering of cake pans as you slide them around the countertop to make space for bowls and spoons. It's about the coldness of flour and butter on your fingertips, the graininess of salt crystals as you pinch them into a bowl of avalanched flour. Baking is about the sweet smells of cinnamon and sugar mingling to bring nostalgic memories of a lax, carefree childhood of apple pies and snickerdoodles. It's about the taste of sensuous melted dark chocolate left in a casually scraped bowl. Baking is, most important, about sharing love and happiness in the form of treats that reflect your changing moods throughout the day—at breakfast time, at three o'clock, and during midnight walks into the kitchen. So roll up your sleeves, blare your favorite music, and preheat your oven. It's time to get your hands into things—to make something deliciously hand made!

# kitchen basics

You don't need a professional kitchen with expensive machinery and baking pans, or even a pantry full of posh exotic ingredients, to make any of the recipes in this book. You need only a few basics, which I point out here—and even some of these, to be honest, you can do without.

# PANS

Buy some or all of the following.

**BUNDT PANS AND/OR TUBE PANS (10 in/25 cm or 9 in/23 cm; with a volume capacity of between 10 and 12 cups/2.3 and 2.8 L):**

It's good to have at least one on hand, especially if you plan to make a Lemon–Poppy Seed Drizzle Cake (page 156). These pans are also great for those times when you'd like to add pizzazz to your cakes; they add great shape and height.

**GLASS OR METAL PIE PANS (9 in/23 cm):**

The best time to stockpile these is during the holidays, when supermarkets tend to sell pie pans quite cheaply. Two or three should serve you well, depending on how much pie you like to bake.

**LOAF PANS (8 by 4 in/20 by 10 cm and 9 by 5 in/23 by-12 cm):**

Essential, especially if you like bread and loaf cakes. At least one of each is a must, but two of each is even better.

**LOOSE-BOTTOM FLUTED TART PAN (9 in/23 cm or 10 in/25 cm):**

This is a great choice, especially when you're not in the mood to crimp dough; a fancy edge is as simple as laying the dough into the pan and pressing it into the gorgeous fluted side.

**RECTANGULAR BAKING PAN (9 by 13 in/23 by 33 cm):**

If you like Swiss rolls (see page 137), you definitely need one of these.

**RIMMED BAKING SHEETS, COOKIE SHEETS, OR SHEET PANS (13 by 18 in/33 by 46 cm):**

You need at least two. These pans are so crucial because they are so versatile. The listed size is the standard for restaurants, but they come in a plethora of other sizes; buy one that fits in your oven. If you can, invest in baking sheets that are sturdy—ones that have weight to them, as they distribute heat evenly and make for great baked goods. Calphalon, Nordic Ware, Chicago Metallic, and Matfer Bourgeat all do a wonderful job with their baking sheets and pans, but you needn't dig deeply to pay for quality baking sheets. Commercial baking sheets from baking supply shops are fantastic and cheaper than brand-name ones.

**ROUND CAKE PANS (8 in/20 cm or 9 in/23 cm):**

You want at least two, but if you like tall cakes, buy four.

**SQUARE BAKING PAN (8 in/20 cm or 9 in/23 cm):**

Either size will do. This pan, after the rimmed baking sheets and round cake pans, is your most important baking tool, especially if you like brownies and blondies as much as I do.

**12-CUP MUFFIN PANS:**

You need two. Whether you're making cupcakes, muffins, or minibreads, these pans are standbys. The standard size of each cup is about 3 in/8 cm in diameter and 1 in/3 cm in depth, or 7 Tbsp/ 100 ml in volume.

# APPLIANCES

**DIGITAL KITCHEN SCALE:**

This is a necessity in all kitchens. Not only does using a scale cut down on dishwashing; it gives you constant accuracy while you're baking, and that is important in many recipes. Digital scales come in all shapes and sizes and are available almost everywhere online and in specialty and kitchenware stores—you can get a good-quality, reliable one for about the same price as a set of good-quality measuring cups. A scale with an 11-lb/4-kg maximum and an option to switch from grams to kilograms and ounces to pounds is a good choice. I developed all the recipes in this book using a kitchen scale (mine is an Oxo with a stainless-steel top, which is great when I'm measuring things into a hot pan) and standard measuring cups. Remember: A gram is the same everywhere in the world, but a cupful of an ingredient can vary from person to person because everyone can measure a cupful of something differently (I explain this more on page 16).

**FOOD PROCESSOR:**

I have an 11-cup/2.5-L Cuisinart food processor, and though I used it many a time for speed mixing in this book's recipes, it's not indispensable.

**HANDHELD ELECTRIC MIXER:**

Even if you're only an occasional baker, this is a requirement, especially if you plan to bake cookies or mix batters. It's a great alternative to a stand mixer (though you can't knead dough with it). There are many brands of mixers out there, and any one of them will do—you just need something that can stand a little kitchen brutality once in a while.

**STAND MIXER:**

If you bake regularly, this is a worthy investment. A stand mixer not only makes mixing and beating ingredients less messy, it also makes the process more pleasurable. I own a KitchenAid; Cuisinart, Breville, and DeLonghi make stand mixers that are of great quality as well.

**TIMER:**

Though you don't need to physically go out to buy one, as most cell phones and microwaves have a timer function, a real timer is perfect if you don't want to click through menus to set it up. A digital one or an old manual one with a loud bell is a good choice—avoid cheap dollar-store ones, as they tend to be moody.

# OTHER EQUIPMENT

**CAKE SKEWERS:**

Buy cheap bamboo skewers, bamboo toothpicks, or a thin metal cake tester. I use small bamboo skewers to test my baked goods, but choose the option you like best.

**CAKE SPATULAS:**

Use these to frost cakes, transfer baked goods, and so on. A large offset spatula will do; a large flat cake spatula is also handy, but not entirely necessary. (By the way, I've left pastry bags and fancy frosting tips off this list because this book is about home baking, not creating wedding-worthy cakes—though if you're really good with a spatula, you can make a spectacular cake!)

**COOKIE AND BISCUIT CUTTERS:**

A round one, with either fluted or plain edges, is crucial to have on hand—especially for biscuit making. Though plastic ones are usually the way to go because they have neat edges for easy cutting and are easy to clean, there are some great metal cookie cutters worth picking up, too. I have a modest (well, I think it is anyway) collection of about two hundred cookie cutters that I've gathered over the years. Each time I see great, fun-shaped cookie cutters on sale at the grocery store or the kitchen supply shop, I buy a few and store them with my other cookie cutters in shoe box–size see-through plastic containers.

**GRATERS:**

Get a box grater and a fine-toothed rasp zester; I swear by the Microplane brand. Their products are a bit on the pricey end, but they're a worthwhile investment, especially for effortless zesting during the holidays when we're usually baking the most. I know many people who say they can't live without theirs.

**KNIVES:**

An 8-in/20-cm chef's knife; a small, reliable paring knife; and a long, sharp, serrated bread knife (about 12 in/30 cm long) are three good knives to have around.

**MEASURING CUPS AND SPOONS:**

Metal or ceramic ones are best for measuring dry ingredients; plastic tends to bend and change shape, so I'd suggest avoiding plastic measuring utensils no matter how durable some might seem. Amco and Oxo make accurate and reliable measuring cups and spoons. For liquid measures, glass is best; I find Pyrex to be the most reliable.

**METAL OR PLASTIC DOUGH/ BENCH SCRAPERS:**

These are used for all sorts of kitchen scraping and for bread making. They're very affordable and an indispensable tool in a baker's kitchen.

**MIXING BOWLS:**

Find metal or glass (preferably heat-resistant) ones that nest inside one another for easy storage. If you're a first-time baker, a large, a medium, and a small bowl will do you good.

**OVEN:**

It's obvious to point out that you need an oven. But you need one that is reliable, meaning that if you set it to 350°F/180°C, you can count on it achieving precisely that temperature. It's a good idea to keep an oven thermometer (get one anywhere: from supermarkets and kitchenware shops to drugstores and hardware stores) in the oven to make sure it is accurate. If your oven is wonky, call in a repairman to have it calibrated.

**OVEN MITTS:**

A couple of good pairs of these. No explanation necessary.

### PASTRY BRUSHES:

These are essential for brushing on glazes, greasing cake pans, and brushing flour off doughs. I have several with natural bristles (the Matfer Bourgeat flat pastry brush is my favorite among the natural-bristled bunch because its bristles don't fall off, like many other brands' do). Nylon and silicone bristles are other options. I'm partial to my fine-bristled silicone brushes from Oxo, too, as they're heat-resistant at high temperatures, the bristles don't clump at all (like their natural- and nylon-bristled cousins do), making for even glazing—even on delicate pastries.

### ROLLING PINS:

For rolling dough, smashing cookies and crackers to fine smithereens, and scaring away uncontrollable cookie thieves, a rolling pin is necessary for this book's recipes. You'll be happy if you invest in a good one. There's an endless array of rolling pins out there. I have two, a wooden French rolling pin and a wooden roller type with fixed handles on the ends. Glass, marble, granite, silicone, and nylon are other options you might like. Go with one that works for you.

### SIEVES:

Purchase fine- or medium-mesh ones, preferably. I find these to be indispensable. It's worthwhile to invest in a couple of strong stainless-steel ones, as wire sieves easily break and become misshapen.

### HEAT-RESISTANT AND FLEXIBLE SILICONE SPATULAS:

Buy a couple of sizes. You need them for mixing and for scraping bowls. Le Creuset and GIR (a new brand) make excellent spatulas. I find that all silicone spatulas, no matter how well I clean them, absorb (for a while, at least) the odor of the food with which I last used them. Be sure to separate your spatulas if you plan to use them for cooking and baking—for example, a curried Nutella Shortbread Sandwich Cookie, though an interesting idea, would not exactly be good eating.

### WHISKS:

A classic balloon whisk is vital, especially when you have to whisk dry ingredients together in a bowl.

### WIRE COOLING RACKS:

You want something sturdy—racks large enough on which to cool freshly baked cakes and cookies. You can find these just about everywhere: discount stores, specialty shops, kitchen supply shops, and, of course, online.

# INGREDIENTS

Here are the baking ingredients you should keep in your cupboard and refrigerator most of the time. None of them should be troublesome to find, but if you can't locate them, see the Resources section near the back of the book, where I provide specific places to find certain ingredients.

- All-purpose flour: bleached or unbleached
- Almond extract (pure)
- Baking powder—the aluminum-free kind. The other kind available is made with sodium aluminum sulfate and it makes baked goods taste bitter, and that isn't good for most baking, especially Angelic Biscuits (page 193), which can call for large amounts of this ingredient.
- Baking soda or sodium bicarbonate
- Bread flour
- Brown sugar or muscovado sugar, both light and dark varieties
- Cake flour (not self-rising)
- Chocolate chips: dark and milk
- Confectioners' sugar—also known as powdered sugar and icing sugar
- Cream: heavy cream or whipping cream (light or heavy). If you're in the United Kingdom, double cream is another option.
- Cream cheese
- Demerara or turbinado sugar—the latter is easier to find in the United States.
- Fine-grain sea salt
- Golden syrup or light corn syrup: Golden syrup—for frostings and for dribbling onto buttered Cream Scones (page 22)—is readily available in the United Kingdom and at most supermarkets in the United States, but light corn syrup works just as well in the other recipes in this book.
- Granulated sugar and/or natural cane sugar
- Ground cinnamon
- Ground nutmeg
- Honey
- Ice cream: homemade vanilla bean or Häagen-Dazs
- Jams: strawberry and raspberry
- Large eggs
- Nuts—keep these in the freezer, as they tend to go rancid rather quickly. Buy walnuts, pistachios, macadamia nuts, hazelnuts, almonds, pecans—or whichever type you like.
- Oil: sunflower, canola, vegetable—anything neutral tasting
- Peanut butter
- Raisins: regular and/or golden (sultanas)
- Rolled oats (not the quick-cooking kind)
- Sour cream
- Unsalted butter—throughout the book, recipes call for room-temperature butter. Some kitchens have higher temperatures than others, causing the butter you've left out on the counter to be mushy and oily. In order for butter to be at room temperature, leave it out for about 30 minutes or as necessary depending on the temperature of your kitchen. Proper room-temperature butter should give easily, but not entirely, when pressed with a clean finger. It should be able to hold its shape.
- Unsweetened cocoa powder: natural and Dutch-processed
- Vanilla extract (pure) and/or vanilla bean paste—the best quality you can afford. I like Nielsen-Massey.
- Whole milk (full-fat)
- Yeast: quick-rising (instant) and dry active
- Yogurt

# before you begin

If you are like me, you probably don't like being told what to do. But if you skip over tips like the ones I give here, you could mess up while making the recipes, which I have done on more than one occasion. So before you run to the kitchen and start mixing ingredients, let's go through a few pointers.

**READ EACH RECIPE ALL THE WAY THROUGH FIRST:**

This will help you to remember ingredients, properly plan dough rises, and avoid any confusion.

**MEASURE ACCURATELY:**

I insist a couple of times in this book that a kitchen scale is a cook's most essential tool (invest in one, if you haven't already). It makes life easier, but if you're into measuring cups, that's okay—I tested all the recipes using the "fluff, pour, and sweep" method. This goes as follows: To properly measure flour, fluff the flour in its container with a spoon, pour the flour into a cup (don't tap the cup, which compacts the flour), and, with the flat side of a knife or another flat object, sweep straight across, flush to the top of the measuring cup. Please don't use liquid measuring cups to measure dry ingredients—doing so simply creates dreadful inaccuracies.

**USE AN OVEN THERMOMETER:**

I cannot stress this enough. It might seem like a silly investment, but all ovens are not made equal. During the writing of this book, I went from a state-of-the-art calibrated electric oven to an unreliable gas oven with a standard dial that was made at the turn of the past century. Being able to accurately check if your oven is too hot or too cool allows you to adjust your heat accordingly.

**PREHEAT THE OVEN:**

This is a requirement no matter what kind of oven you have. As I mentioned, all ovens are different, and this means that it could take anywhere from 15 minutes to 30 minutes (or sometimes even longer) for your oven to reach the desired temperature. Be sure to plan accordingly.

**ROTATE PANS:**

My fellow gas-oven users, pan rotation is essential for even baking. (It's helpful for electric-oven baking, too, but I can't stress it enough for gas-oven users.) If you're using two pans on two separate racks in the oven, halfway through baking, switch the pans with each other and rotate them 180 degrees. If you're using a single pan, simply rotate it 180 degrees in either direction.

**WATCH BAKING TIMES:**

Time is crucial when it comes to baking. I've provided ranges of baking times in each of the recipes found in this book; the times given are those that have worked for me. My personal baking times usually fall in the middle of all the given baking times, which allows for those with cooler-running ovens to follow the longer baking times and for those whose ovens run hotter than normal to follow the shorter suggested baking times. As a rule of thumb, I visually check the food halfway through baking, and again 5 or so minutes before the "done" time. You should look too; when it appears to be done, then simply check it in the manner the recipe directs you to.

### USE FRESH INGREDIENTS:

We've all been there—a recipe we make on a regular basis ends up failing because it sunk in the middle, didn't rise, or didn't taste as it normally does. The problem could be that you used an ingredient that had expired. Just like most pantry items, flours, yeast, baking soda, and baking powder have expiration dates, so be sure to check them. I keep many of my "exotic" flours (whole wheat, pastry, graham, and almond meal) in the freezer, as these go rancid rather quickly. If your flour smells like wet paint, that means it's gone bad and you need to replace it. Replace your baking soda and baking powder every six months or so after opening, even if they haven't reached their printed expiration dates, and check them for freshness every so often. To check if baking soda is fresh, add a scant teaspoonful of white vinegar to a teaspoonful of baking soda in a small bowl. For baking powder, add a teaspoonful of hot water to a teaspoonful of baking powder in a small bowl. In both cases, if it fizzes, all is well.

### USE PARCHMENT PAPER:

When a recipe calls for lining a pan with parchment paper, please use it. It's a sad business when you make the effort to bake a cake and it then refuses to come out of the pan, or when cookies come out of the oven with burnt edges and uncooked centers. This piece of paper can make all the difference because it not only allows for even baking, but it allows you to release your baked goods from the pan without having to worry about sticking.

### HAVE FUN!

Every recipe in this book leaves plenty of room for you to be creative and to adapt the ingredients to your liking. Don't go as far as to swap out flours (although I do offer alternatives in some recipes) or adjust the leavenings unless you absolutely know what you're doing. However, when it comes to accompaniments—the complementing adornments in the recipes—choose to do what you like. There are near-endless combinations of adaptations you can make to these recipes. If you feel that a pouring of Classic Chocolate Ganache (page 148) would be much better on the Everyday Chocolate Cake (page 142) than the Easy Cocoa Frosting I list there, go for it. Or top your Everyday Brownies (page 123) with a layer of the same ganache and a smattering of pistachio nuts. Divide each layer of your Caribbean Princess Cake (page 149) in half and alternately fill the layers with guava and dulce de leche. Or glob softened ice cream onto your Blue Teeth Blueberry Pie (page 59) without a second thought. Trust your instincts and your taste buds—they'll serve you well.

# rise and shine

When visiting with my dad's side of the family, you'll immediately learn that breakfast is an important meal to eat together—whether we're biting into just-out-of-the-oven Blueberry Corn Muffins (page 20) smothered in softened butter, scooping spoonfuls of Strawberry Crumble (page 29) into dishes, or sitting next to one another in companionable silence behind bowls of Cinnamon-Raisin Granola (page 48) festooned with banana slices and covered in yogurt and honey. There's no saying how many of my family are around at a certain time, but we make sure to have breakfast together. It might be prepared the night before, or made the morning of, but breakfast—no matter how simple it is—is a big deal to us. In a world where a bit of sweetness is especially required during any weekday, weekend, or holiday morning breakfast, these recipes are quite fitting to serve alongside your usual eggs, toast, and warm beverage.

I use Quick Puff Pastry (page 37) quite a bit in this section, as I find it versatile and appropriate for breakfast treats, but there's something in here for everyone, from Whatchamacallit Apple Crumble (page 32) to Chocolate Puffs (page 42) to the Forgetaboutit Cinnamon Rolls (page 25). Delicious.

# BLUEBERRY CORN MUFFINS

**MAKES 9 MUFFINS**

**These muffins burst at their seams with blueberries. They have sugar-crusted crunchy tops and a beautifully textured and moist inner crumb. They're best eaten on the same day that you make them, slightly warm and with a pat of butter, but they're still lovely the next day.**

**1 cup/120 g whole-wheat pastry flour or all-purpose flour**

**½ cup/70 g yellow cornmeal**

**1¾ tsp baking powder**

**¼ tsp fine-grain sea salt**

**6 Tbsp/85 g unsalted butter, at room temperature**

**½ cup/100 g natural cane sugar or granulated sugar**

**1 large egg, at room temperature**

**¾ cup/180 ml full-fat plain yogurt, at room temperature**

**½ tsp finely grated lemon zest**

**1 cup/125 g fresh or frozen blueberries**

**Heaping 1 Tbsp granulated sugar for sprinkling**

Position a rack in the center of the oven. Preheat the oven to 400°F/200°C. Line a muffin tin with nine paper liners, or liberally butter each cup.

In a medium bowl, whisk together the flour, cornmeal, baking powder, and salt. Set aside.

In a large bowl with a handheld mixer, or in the bowl of a stand mixer fitted with the paddle attachment, beat together the butter and cane sugar on medium speed until light in color and fluffy in consistency, about 5 minutes. Stop the machine, scrape down the sides of the bowl, add the egg, and beat on medium-low speed until well incorporated.

Add the yogurt and lemon zest. Turn the speed to low, add the flour mixture all at once, and mix until some of the flour is incorporated into the batter.

With the machine off, gently fold in the blueberries with a silicone spatula until the flour and berries are just incorporated into the batter. Don't overmix.

Evenly fill the nine muffin cups and sprinkle each with some of the granulated sugar. Bake for 24 to 28 minutes, rotating the pan halfway through baking, until the tops are golden brown and a toothpick inserted into the center of each muffin comes out clean or with a few stray crumbs attached. Let the muffins cool in the pan for about 6 minutes, just until the pan is cool to the touch, before transferring to a wire rack to cool slightly (or completely, if you prefer cool muffins) before serving.

### note

It may be unusual to mix the batter only until some of the flour is incorporated and then add the blueberries—you'll see flour remaining on the surface of the batter. My explanation: In most recipes, if you use frozen blueberries, you need to toss the blueberries in flour so they won't stain the batter and sink to its bottom. I find that mixing in the berries in the fashion that I described works just as well and saves you from washing another bowl (you're welcome).

# CREAM SCONES

**MAKES ABOUT 9 SCONES**

**The very first time I baked scones for my mother, she cautiously bit into one, saying, "I really don't like scones." But almost immediately, she smiled. Like many people, my mother had memories of scones best described as dull, heavy, or dry. Instead these were buttery, moist, and tender. The secret to good scones is to handle the dough as little as possible and to use cold ingredients to achieve flaky layers; that's about it! These are proper scones—ones that will heal anyone's memories of bad scones. Friends often ask me to make this recipe, especially during the summertime, to accompany the many jars of handmade Back of a Napkin jam (see page 107) that I make.**

## CREAM DOUGH

**2½ cups/300 g all-purpose flour**

**5 Tbsp/65 g granulated sugar**

**1 Tbsp baking powder**

**¼ tsp fine-grain sea salt**

**6 Tbsp/85 g cold unsalted butter, cut into ½-in/12-mm cubes**

**1 cup/240 ml heavy (whipping) cream**

**1 large egg, cold**

**½ tsp pure vanilla extract**

## SUGAR TOPPING

**1 large egg**

**½ tsp granulated sugar**

**Pinch of fine-grain sea salt**

**Demerara sugar for sprinkling**

**TO MAKE THE DOUGH:** In a large bowl, whisk together the flour, sugar, baking powder, and salt. Add the butter and rub it into the flour mixture with your fingertips, two butter knives, or a pastry blender until the mixture resembles coarse meal and no pieces of butter are larger than a pea.

In a glass measuring cup, beat together the cream, egg, and vanilla. Pour the cream mixture into the flour mixture, and stir until a dough forms.

Lightly flour a clean work surface and turn out the dough, gently kneading it onto itself for 10 seconds.

Pat the dough into a square about ¾ in/2 cm thick and let it rest for 15 minutes. Position a rack in the center of the oven. Preheat the oven to 425°F/220°C. Line a rimmed baking sheet with parchment paper.

Once the oven has preheated, use a knife to cut the dough into nine squares and put them on the prepared baking sheet. Or use a round cutter or the rim of a glass dipped in flour to punch out circles of dough. Be sure to cut them as closely to one another as possible; you should get six rounds, and when you pat the dough back together (it doesn't need to be a square this time), you should be able to get three more rounds. Avoid rerolling the dough during this second stage, as this will result in tough scones.

**TO MAKE THE TOPPING:** In a small bowl, beat together the egg, granulated sugar, and salt. Lightly brush the tops of the dough pieces with the mixture and wait 1 minute until the topping sets. Sprinkle the tops with Demerara sugar (about ½ tsp per scone). Bake for 13 to 18 minutes, until the scones are golden brown. Be sure to rotate the pan halfway through baking.

Allow the scones to sit in the pan for 2 minutes before transferring to a wire rack to cool for 5 to 10 minutes more.

Serve the same day.

*continued*

## notes

These scones are enjoyable plain, with jam, with a pat of butter, or with a bit of Devonshire cream. Or add 1 cup/125 g of fresh or frozen berries (don't thaw them) to the dough—your results will turn out like the pictured scones.

We have a split vote in my household on which way the berries should be incorporated into the dough—sandwiched between two layers, or kneaded into it.

The first method: Roll out the dough into a 7-by-12-in/17-by-30-cm rectangle and place the berries on one side of the dough, leaving a ½-in/12-mm border. Fold the dough in half and press down on it with your hands until the dough is ¾ in/2 cm thick. Proceed to cut. If the berries slide out, just push them back in.

The second method: Simply knead the berries into the dough before you pat it into a square and cut it.

## variations

**RASPBERRY AND DARK CHOCOLATE:** Knead chopped dark chocolate (whatever floats your boat; 2 oz/55 g or thereabouts should be sufficient) into the dough. Add 1 cup/125 g of raspberries by either folding the dough over them or kneading them into the dough.

**CHOCOLATE:** Knead about 2½ oz/70 g of good-quality (54 to 70 percent cacao) chocolate into the dough.

**BLUEBERRY-LEMON OR BLUEBERRY-ORANGE:** Mix 1 tsp of finely grated lemon or orange zest into the flour mixture, and incorporate 1 cup/125 g of fresh or frozen (unthawed) blueberries into the dough.

**RAISIN:** Mix 1 cup/125 g of golden raisins into the dough.

# FORGETABOUTIT CINNAMON ROLLS

**MAKES 18 ROLLS; SERVES 4 TO 6 GREEDY PEOPLE**

**I know nothing better than the sweet, enticing smells of yeast and cinnamon wafting around the house on an early winter morning. These cinnamon rolls, though somewhat time consuming, are well worth the process. You get much-needed therapy from working the dough, and then sweet satisfaction from the finished product. Once they're out of the oven, brush the soft rolls with milk or cream and cover them in delicious Tangy Cream Cheese Frosting—making them, as one of my friends likes to put it, "Forgetaboutit good!"**

## DOUGH

**6 cups/720 g all-purpose flour**

**¾ cup/150 g granulated sugar**

**1 Tbsp quick-rise (instant) yeast**

**1½ tsp fine-grain sea salt**

**1½ cups/360 ml milk, heated to 115°F/45°C (see Note, page 28)**

**5 Tbsp/70 g unsalted butter, melted**

**1 large egg plus 1 large egg yolk, at room temperature**

**2 tsp pure vanilla extract**

## FILLING

**1 cup/200 g packed dark brown sugar**

**3 Tbsp ground cinnamon**

**Pinch of fine-grain sea salt**

**6 Tbsp/85 g unsalted butter, at room temperature**

**Milk, cream, or half-and-half for brushing on the rolls**

**½ recipe Tangy Cream Cheese Frosting (page 28)**

**TO MAKE THE DOUGH:** Lightly oil a large bowl and set it aside.

In the bowl of a stand mixer fitted with the paddle attachment, mix 5 cups/600 g of the flour, the granulated sugar, yeast, and salt together on low speed. With the mixer still running, add the warm milk, butter, whole egg, egg yolk, and vanilla. Continue mixing on low speed for about 4 minutes, occasionally scraping down the sides of the bowl.

At this point, the dough might still be sticky; if this is the case (it usually is for me), add the remaining 1 cup/120 g flour, 1 Tbsp at a time, until the dough begins to form into a ball and pulls away from the sides of the bowl. (You can add more than the reserved amount if necessary.)

On a clean, lightly floured, sturdy surface, knead the dough until it's smooth and springy, about 10 minutes. If the dough is sticky, incorporate a little flour. Once you have kneaded the dough, form it into a round, put it in the oiled bowl, and turn it to coat with oil. Cover the bowl with a clean, damp dish towel. Let it rise in a warm, draft-free place for about 2 hours, or until it has doubled in size.

**TO MAKE THE FILLING:** While the dough is rising, sift into a bowl the brown sugar, cinnamon, and salt. Set this aside.

Deflate the dough (punch it down, really). Transfer the dough to a clean, floured surface and roll it out into an 18-by-14-in/46-by-35.5-cm rectangle. Evenly spread the butter on the dough, followed by the filling. Beginning with a long side, roll the dough into a log, pinching the seam to seal it.

*continued*

Let the dough sit for a minute or so while you liberally butter (or line with parchment paper) two 9-in/23-cm round cake pans. Set them aside.

With the dough log seam-side down, use a sharp knife or unflavored plain dental floss to cut the log into 18 equal pieces, each 1 in/2.5 cm thick. Lay the rolls in the prepared cake pans, cover the pans with a damp, clean cloth, and allow the rolls to rise for about 1 hour, until they double in size. (At this point, after the rolls have risen, you can cover the pans in plastic wrap and put them in the refrigerator overnight or up to 24 hours. When you're ready to bake them, allow them 30 minutes to come to room temperature.)

After the rolls have rested for 45 minutes (or for 15 minutes if the rolls have been refrigerated and are coming to room temperature), position a rack in the center of the oven. Preheat the oven to 375°F/190°C.

Bake the rolls for 18 to 23 minutes, until the tops are a light golden brown and a toothpick or wooden skewer inserted into the center rolls comes out clean. If you tap on the top of the rolls, they should sound hollow.

Once they're out of the oven, brush the rolls lightly with milk. Allow them to cool in the pans for about 10 minutes before frosting them and serving.

### notes

To measure the temperature of the milk, use an instant-read or candy thermometer.

If you prefer, you can knead the dough in a stand mixer fitted with the paddle attachment, on the lowest setting, for 5 to 6 minutes instead of manually kneading it by hand. Because there is so much flour in this recipe, though, be sure to refer to your stand mixer's instructions beforehand to make sure it's safe for your mixer to do this job.

## TANGY CREAM CHEESE FROSTING

**MAKES ABOUT ½ CUP/200 G**

**This frosting is tangy and sweet, but not intensely so—it's the perfect accompaniment to cinnamon rolls, but it's also fantastic on cake. If you'd like, leave out the orange zest and substitute milk for the orange juice to make a plain cream cheese frosting.**

**½ cup/50 g confectioners' sugar**

**4 oz/115 g cream cheese, at room temperature**

**1 Tbsp unsalted butter, at room temperature**

**1 tsp orange juice**

**½ tsp finely grated orange zest**

**Pinch of fine-grain sea salt**

In a medium bowl, or in the bowl of a stand mixer fitted with the paddle attachment, combine all the ingredients and beat on medium speed until they are smooth and well mixed.

# STRAWBERRY CRUMBLE

**SERVES 4 TO 6**

**My family and I love eating this crumble cold, straight out of the refrigerator, for breakfast. I make it the night before, let it cool a bit, spoon it into small jars, and keep it cold overnight. This recipe transforms lackluster winter strawberries into an intensely flavorful crumble appropriate for weekend breakfasts or desserts. The magic happens under a blanket of buttery oat topping freckled with poppy seeds. After about half an hour of oven time, the berries are transformed into succulent, berrily intense (it's a technical term) explosions of flavor that bring memories of summer to me: warm, verdant fields and pillows of clouds scattered across the azure sky.**

### STRAWBERRY FILLING

**1 lb/455 g fresh strawberries, hulled**

**3½ Tbsp/45 g vanilla sugar (see Note)**

**¼ cup/30 g all-purpose flour**

### CRUMBLE TOPPING

**1 cup/120 g all-purpose flour**

**1½ tsp poppy seeds (optional but suggested)**

**1 tsp baking powder**

**¼ tsp fine-grain sea salt**

**6 Tbsp/85 g cold unsalted butter, cut into small chunks**

**1¼ cups/195 g rolled oats (not quick-cooking)**

**5 Tbsp/65 g turbinado sugar or Demerara sugar**

Position a rack in the center of the oven. Preheat the oven to 400°F/200°C.

**TO MAKE THE FILLING:** Put the strawberries in a 9-in/23-cm ungreased cake pan or baking dish.

Sprinkle the vanilla sugar evenly over the strawberries, followed by the flour. Give the pan a slight shake to mix the ingredients a bit, and set it aside.

**TO MAKE THE TOPPING:** In a medium mixing bowl, whisk together the flour, poppy seeds (if using), baking powder, and salt. Rub the butter into the flour mixture with your fingertips until the mixture resembles pale oatmeal (you can do this with a pastry blender or two butter knives). With a fork, stir in the oats and turbinado sugar.

Evenly cover the strawberries with the crumble mixture and bake for 28 to 32 minutes. The crumble is ready when the topping is slightly bronzed and pinkish-red juices are bubbling out through the crumble topping.

Serve warm, at room temperature, or cold from the fridge.

### *notes*

Taste the berries first to see how sweet they are (don't use wild strawberries; they are too delicate). Adjust the amount of sugar you use accordingly.

If you don't have premade vanilla sugar on hand, use 3½ Tbsp/45 g natural cane or granulated sugar and 1 Tbsp vanilla bean paste or pure vanilla extract. See Resources (page 200) for places to find premade vanilla sugar.

You can make this dish ahead of time: Assemble the entire crumble up to a day in advance. Wrap the pan well in plastic wrap, put it in the refrigerator, and when you're ready, bake as directed, allowing a few extra minutes of baking time. This dish is also superb when served for dessert with big scoops of vanilla ice cream, a heaping dollop of Billowy Whipped Cream (page 65), or a generous glug of cold heavy (whipping) cream.

# WHATCHAMA-CALLIT APPLE CRUMBLE

**SERVES 4 TO 6**

**Is it a crumble or is it a crisp? If you were to search the Internet for the difference between the two, you'd find endless Web pages filled with conflicting information and crumble-versus-crisp smack-downs. Instead, let's talk about how this is actually a close cousin to apple pie. Here, oat-based topping adds texture, and cinnamon gives the crumble warmth. After a short time in the oven, the crumble offers apple pie flavors in a simple breakfast form.**

## APPLE FILLING

**2 tsp lemon juice**

**4 apples; 2 sweet and 2 sour (see Note)**

**2 Tbsp granulated sugar**

**1/8 tsp ground cinnamon**

**Pinch of fine-grain sea salt**

## CRUMBLE TOPPING

**1 cup/120 g all-purpose flour**

**3/4 tsp baking powder**

**1/4 tsp fine-grain sea salt**

**Pinch of ground cinnamon**

**6 Tbsp/85 g cold unsalted butter, cut into small cubes**

**1 1/2 cups/150 g rolled oats (not quick-cooking)**

**1/3 cup/70 g turbinado sugar or Demerara sugar**

Position a rack in the center of the oven. Preheat the oven to 425°F/200°C. Butter an 11-by-7-in/28-by-17-cm baking pan or a baking dish that holds about 2 qt/2 L.

**TO MAKE THE FILLING:** Pour the lemon juice into a large mixing bowl. Peel, core, and slice the apples and add them to the bowl, tossing them in the juice as you work (this will prevent the apples from browning).

Mix in the granulated sugar, cinnamon, and salt. Carefully toss with the apples, then spread them evenly into the prepared baking pan. Set the pan aside.

**TO MAKE THE TOPPING:** In a medium bowl, whisk together the flour, baking powder, salt, and cinnamon. Rub the butter into the flour mixture with your fingertips until the mixture resembles pale oatmeal (you can do this with a pastry blender or two butter knives). With a fork, stir in the oats and turbinado sugar.

Evenly cover the apples with the topping mixture and set the baking pan on a large rimmed baking sheet. Bake for 20 to 25 minutes; the crumble is ready when the topping is slightly browned and the apples are soft.

Serve warm.

### notes

I like to mix Rome apples (which are sweet) and Granny Smith apples (which are tart) for this crumble, but use any equivalent baking apples.

Just like the Strawberry Crumble (page 29), this is great for dessert, too. It's obligatory to serve it with a hearty scoop of vanilla ice cream. And on the subject of pairing vanilla ice cream with handmade baked goods, I do claim to be an authority. Well, not a quarreling one—just a thoughtful one here to help enhance your eating experience.

# MAXINES

MAKES ABOUT 36 MAXINES

After months of constant trial and error, I grew frustrated with the results of my experiments with madeleines. Some would sink, some had the crumb of a dishwashing sponge, and some would stick to the pan. However, after several more trials and frustrations, I developed this lovely recipe; they aren't too different than a traditional madeleine, aside from the name and the use of brown butter and a few other nontraditional ingredients. After knowing of my frustrations during the early development of this recipe, my friends Hannah and Lauren said, "Why not call them Maxines?"—a name that preserves the classiness and appeal of madeleines, but doesn't outright call them such to prevent any confusion that these might, in fact, be traditional.

The batter is flavored with nutty brown butter, almond meal (which also adds to the Maxines' moistness), a bit of vanilla, and a healthy pinch of lemon zest—it all comes together in a cinch. No complicated mixing is required, as it is in most madeleine recipes. The batter lasts a couple of days in the refrigerator (covered, of course), which allows you to bake tea cakes within a moment's notice. I like to serve them for breakfast with strongly brewed black tea, lightly sweetened and with just enough milk to turn the dark liquid into a caramel-colored potion.

**½ cup/100 g granulated sugar**

**½ cup/60 g whole-wheat pastry flour or all-purpose flour**

**½ cup/40 g almond meal or ⅓ cup/40 g all-purpose flour**

**1¼ tsp baking powder**

**Pinch of fine-grain sea salt**

**2 large eggs, at room temperature, lightly beaten**

**¾ tsp pure vanilla extract**

**½ tsp finely grated lemon zest**

**10 Tbsp/140 g Brown Butter (recipe follows)**

**Confectioners' sugar for dusting**

Position a rack in the center of the oven. Preheat the oven to 400°F/200°C.

Liberally butter a madeleine pan with 12 molds. Dust the molds with flour and turn the pan over to tap out any excess flour (do so over the sink; it makes for easier clean-up).

In a large bowl, whisk together the granulated sugar, pastry flour, almond meal, baking powder, and salt. Use a wooden spoon or sturdy silicone spatula to mix in the eggs, vanilla, and lemon zest until incorporated. Pour the brown butter along the inner side of the bowl and stir until it's just combined.

Spoon the batter into the prepared molds, filling them no more than three-quarters full. Bake for 7 to 10 minutes (or 5 to 8 minutes for smaller ones), until the Maxines are golden and well risen, have a beautiful bump in the center, and are springy to the touch.

Once they're out of the oven, immediately unmold the Maxines and allow them to cool on a wire rack. Clean and prepare the pan again to make more Maxines, or cover and refrigerate the batter for up to 2 days and bake as needed.

Serve with a dusting of confectioners' sugar.

continued

### note

To make these cookies, you need a madeleine baking pan—there's no way around this. There's a huge range of these pans on the market. I use a metal one, as it gives the cookies a beautiful, even color; however, there are many silicone varieties that work just as well. If you are using a silicone pan, keep in mind you still have to butter and flour the molds (the same holds true if you're using a nonstick metal pan).

# BROWN BUTTER

**Brown butter, or beurre noisette (French for "hazelnut butter"), is butter that is cooked until it is amber colored and nutty smelling. It's delicious in baked goods, especially Maxines (page 34). If you're making brown butter to substitute in recipes like the Everyday Brownies (a good idea; see page 123), or the Nancy Drew Blondies (page 129), you'll need 1 cup plus 4 Tbsp/280 g butter for the brownies and 7½ Tbsp/105 g for the blondies.**

Line a sieve with a paper towel or coffee filter. If using the latter, gently run the filter under hot water for a couple of seconds to get rid of any factory residues and to allow the filter to sit in the sieve better; tap gently to get rid of any excess water. Put the sieve over a bowl.

Cube the butter (whatever amount the recipe calls for) and put it in a heavy-bottom saucepan over medium heat until the butter is the color of amber maple syrup and gives off a nutty scent and there are amber-colored butter solids at the bottom of the pan, about 20 minutes.

Immediately pour the brown butter into the lined sieve, using a silicone spatula to scrape every last bit out of the saucepan.

Brown butter will keep in an airtight container in the refrigerator for up to 2 weeks.

# QUICK PUFF PASTRY

**MAKES ABOUT 1 LB/455 G**

**Many chefs say that it's too difficult to make your own puff pastry at home and that you should only purchase it ready-made. What if I told you it is actually simple and well worth the work, especially when you use this recipe, which you can combine and roll out in less than 15 minutes? It results in beautifully puffy and flaky pastry. No more will you have to spend insane amounts of money on prepared puff pastry. Use the photographs on pages 38–39 as a visual reference, and let's begin!**

**2 cups plus 1 Tbsp/250 g all-purpose flour**

**¼ tsp fine-grain sea salt**

**1 cup plus 2 Tbsp/250 g cold unsalted butter, cut into ⅓-in/8-mm cubes**

**⅔ cup/165 ml ice-cold water (you probably won't need all of this)**

In a large bowl, whisk together the flour and salt. Put the butter in the bowl and put the bowl in the freezer for 10 to 15 minutes.

Once chilled, quickly separate the chunks of butter with your fingertips. Use a butter knife to briefly chop the butter into the flour, just enough to coat the butter with flour *(1)*.

Drop the contents of the bowl onto a clean work surface—preferably a marble board or metal counter *(2)*. (A chilled rimmed baking sheet placed upside-down on a damp dish towel works well, too.) Form a well in the middle of the pile of flour and butter. Dribble in 2 to 3 Tbsp of the ice-cold water *(3)*. Quickly mix the water into the flour mixture with your fingertips (spread them a bit apart, as if you were using your hand as a whisk).

You can test the mixture by gently squeezing a small handful. The dough should hold together without crumbling *(4)*. If it doesn't, keep dribbling on water, 2 to 3 Tbsp at a time, until a dough starts to form. Remember to work quickly and to use your fingertips.

Briskly knead the dough onto itself for 15 seconds until the dough holds together.

Using a bench or dough scraper or your hands, form the dough into a rough 4-by-4-in/10-by-10-cm square. Wrap the dough in plastic wrap, and place it in the refrigerator for about 30 minutes, until firm. Then roll out the dough into a 15-by-8-in/38-by-20-cm rectangle *(5)*. Fold the short ends over the middle (as if you were folding a letter) to make three layers *(6)*. This is the first turn.

Rotate the entire rectangle of dough 90 degrees, flip it over (seam-side down; this is where the top of the folds is), and roll it away from you (not side to side) into a 15-by-4-in/38-by-10-cm rectangle *(7)*. Fold the short ends over the middle to make three layers again *(8)*. This is the second turn.

Wrap the dough in plastic wrap and refrigerate it for 30 minutes. (If it isn't hot and humid in your kitchen and you're working quickly, you can skip this refrigeration step and immediately go on to the next two turns.)

Repeat the process of folding and rotating the dough to create the third and fourth turns. Wrap the dough in plastic wrap. Refrigerate it for at least 30 minutes (or up to 3 days) before you use it.

## *notes*

This is one recipe where having a kitchen scale comes in handy. It gives you absolute precision and you don't have to dirty as many dishes.

The dough can be frozen for up to 2 months. Just wrap it well in plastic wrap, put it in a freezer-safe bag, and thaw it out in the refrigerator before use.

2
6

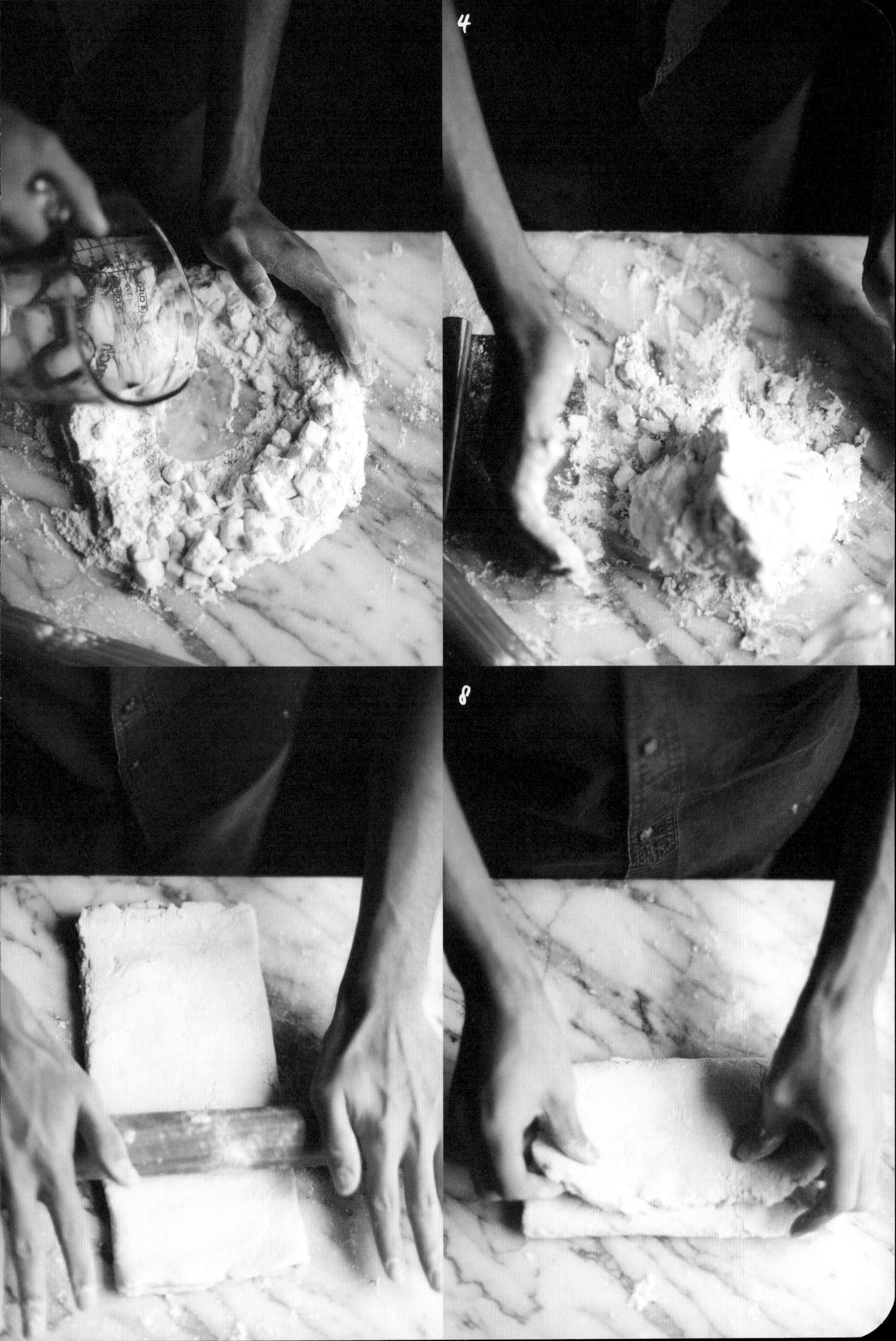
4
8

# BUTTERFLY COOKIES

**MAKES ABOUT 20 COOKIES**

**These cookies evoke many memories of my childhood breakfasts with my grandmother. Each morning I visited her, she'd turn the kettle on, brew strong tea, and take out a package of sweet, flaky heart-shaped cookies wrapped in a beige plastic bag. We'd slowly eat our way through half of the package, carefully dipping the cookies into the piping-hot milky tea. As we nibbled, bits of flaky pastry floated around in the tea, a delicious encouragement to drink it to the very dregs.**

**½ cup/100 g granulated sugar**
**Pinch of fine-grain sea salt**
**½ recipe Quick Puff Pastry (page 37) or 8 oz/225 g store-bought puff pastry**

Position a rack in the center of the oven. Preheat the oven to 425°F/220°C.

Line an 18-by-13-in/46-by-32.5-cm rimmed baking sheet with parchment paper. In a small bowl, mix together the sugar and salt.

On a clean surface, pour out about ¼ cup/50 g of the sugar mixture. Put the puff pastry on top of the sugar and roll it out into a 10-by-13-in/25-by-32.5-cm rectangle (about ½ in/12 mm thick), incorporating the remaining sugar on top of the pastry. Trim the edges with a sharp knife.

Fold both of the long ends inward so they meet at the center of the pastry. Fold both long sides of the pastry over once more *(1)*, and fold one side of the pastry onto the other, making a thin rectangle *(2)*.

Transfer the pastry to the prepared baking sheet, and put it in the freezer for 10 to 15 minutes until the pastry has firmed up.

Transfer the pastry back to your work surface (it's okay if sugar is left on the surface), slice the pastry into ¼-in/6-mm-wide slices *(3)*, and arrange them, cut-side up, about 2 in/5 cm apart on the baking sheet.

Bake the cookies for 12 to 15 minutes, until golden brown. Remove the pan from the oven, flip the cookies over with a spatula, and bake for an additional 5 to 7 minutes, until the sugar on the cookies is caramelized on the other side.

Transfer the cookies to a wire rack to cool completely *(4)* and serve.

### notes

What's in a name? You might know these cookies by the name of palmiers or palm tree cookies or even elephant ears. For the sake of evoking sweet, resplendent daintiness, I've named them Butterfly Cookies (I'm not trying to reinvent the wheel, but I am trying to update it a bit with a more approachable, appropriate name).

Don't forget that pinch of salt. It makes a big difference in the taste—it helps to enhance the flavors of the cookies so much that it's the difference between a good cookie and a great cookie. And cookies should always be great.

### variations

Mix a heaping 1 tsp of cinnamon into the sugar and salt mixture. For pumpkin pie–spice butterfly cookies, use 1½ tsp store-bought pumpkin spice mix or ¾ tsp cinnamon, ¾ tsp ground ginger, and ⅛ tsp ground nutmeg.

# CHOCOLATE PUFFS

**MAKES 12 PUFFS**

**Imagine this: flaky, bronzed, just-out-of-the-oven triangles of buttery layered pastry oozing rich dark chocolate—and you made them in just under 30 minutes! Call this the cheater's route to making the classic pain au chocolat! It's not exactly a proper croissant, but it's oh-so-much easier to make. No complicated dough making and rolling are required, which is a plus—especially early in the morning. Which chocolate you use in this recipe is entirely up to you; pick a good one that you'd eat on its own. I like to use dark chocolate with cacao ranging from 54 to 70 percent.**

**1 recipe Quick Puff Pastry (page 37) or 1 lb/455 g store-bought puff pastry**

**1 large egg, beaten with a fork**

**5 oz/140 g chocolate, roughly chopped (see Note)**

**Sugar of your choice for sprinkling (see Note)**

**Confectioners' sugar for sprinkling (optional)**

Position a rack in the center of the oven. Preheat the oven to 400°F/200°C. Line a rimmed baking sheet with parchment paper.

Lightly flour a clean work surface. Roll out one-half of the puff pastry dough into a 12-in/30-cm square. Trim the edges so you have a perfect square (or close enough—this is home cooking, where function almost always trumps perfection). Cut the square into six 2-in/5-cm squares.

Brush the edges of the pastry squares with the beaten egg. Working somewhat quickly, place about 1 tsp of the chocolate in one corner (inside the line of beaten egg) of each square. Fold the opposite corner of the square onto the chocolate corner to form a triangle. Lightly press the edges closed and seal them using the tines of a fork (dip the fork in flour so the pastry won't stick to it). Put the triangles on the prepared baking sheet, and repeat the process with the remaining half of the pastry.

Put the baking sheet in the freezer for 10 to 15 minutes, until the triangles are firm. After their short visit to the freezer, make a couple of small slits in the top of each pastry triangle, lightly brush their tops with beaten egg, and evenly sprinkle them with your choice of sugar.

Bake for 12 to 15 minutes, until the triangles are puffed and golden brown. Sprinkle with confectioners' sugar (if the spirit moves you) and serve immediately.

## notes

If you run out of chocolate in the middle of this recipe (this has actually happened to me, though my friends and family might not believe it because of my constant chocolate purchases), worry not. Simply use your favorite jam or preserve as filling—it works just as well and makes a very tasty version of this recipe.

The type of sugar you sprinkle on the pastry before it goes into the oven is entirely up to you. On days when I'm too lazy to rummage in the mess of my pantry, I stick to regular granulated sugar. However, if I feel creative and it's early in the morning, I use turbinado or Demerara sugar for a nice crunchy texture on the pastries—whichever is easier to reach without stuff crashing down.

# GUAVA AND CHEESE PUFFS

**MAKES 8 PUFFS**

**Growing up in a family of two very different cultures taught me that despite the many differences between them, they also have many similarities. More often than not, these similarities are about food. Guava is the winter national fruit of Pakistan, my father's native country. It also is a common fruit of the Dominican Republic, my maternal grandmother's country. It grows throughout the world's tropics and subtropics on low-lying trees near riverbeds. In Pakistan, people usually enjoy the fruit with salt and a combination of spices called masala. In the Dominican Republic, they use the fruit to make everything from beverages to jams to pastries (as in this recipe). Because both sides of my family come from places where guava is adored, it's natural that I love it myself.**

**Here, sweet guava and tangy cream cheese are enclosed in buttery, flaky puff pastry—a combination loved throughout Latin America. This recipe is quick and simple, and once you've made it a few times, you can approximate the amounts instead of measuring precisely.**

**1 recipe Quick Puff Pastry (page 37) or 1 lb/455 g store-bought puff pastry**

**1 large egg, beaten with a fork**

**4 oz/115 g guava paste, mashed (see Note)**

**4 oz/115 g cold cream cheese, cut into 8 equal slices**

**¼ cup/50 g granulated sugar**

Position a rack in the center of the oven. Preheat the oven to 425°F/220°C. Line a rimmed baking sheet with parchment paper.

Lightly flour a clean work surface, and roll out one half of the puff pastry into a 10-in/25-cm square. Trim the edges and cut the dough into four equal-size squares.

Brush the edges of the pastry squares with the beaten egg. Working somewhat quickly, place about 1 Tbsp of the guava paste and 1 slice of the cream cheese in one corner (inside the line of beaten egg) of each square and sprinkle with 1 tsp of the sugar. Fold the opposite corner of the square onto the guava corner to form a triangle. Lightly press the edges together and seal them using the tines of a fork (dip the fork in flour so the pastry won't stick to it). Put the triangles on the prepared baking sheet, and repeat the process with the remaining half of the pastry.

Put the baking sheet in the freezer for 10 to 15 minutes, until the triangles are firm. After their short visit to the freezer, make a couple of small slits in the top of each pastry triangle, lightly brush their tops with the beaten egg, and evenly sprinkle them with the remaining sugar.

Bake for 13 to 17 minutes, until the triangles are puffed and golden brown. Allow them to cool for at least 20 minutes before serving.

## note

New York and New Jersey—the places where I grew up and live now—are not exactly the best climate for growing guava, so I've used guava paste in this recipe. It's easy to find at most grocery stores. I've even managed to find it in my middle-of-nowhere town in New Jersey. It is usually located in the Latin or ethnic food aisle, and most often it comes in either a rectangular block wrapped in plastic or in a round tin about the size of a salad plate. Don't confuse this form of guava with the jarred kind, which is actually a jelly. Though guava jelly is delicious spread on warm buttered toast, avoid using it for baking.

ROGERS

# DUTCH BABY PANCAKE

**SERVES 2 TO 4, DEPENDING ON THEIR HUNGER LEVEL**

**The very first time I heard about a Dutch baby pancake was on trash television. I'm not one to watch much television, but when I was a high school student, any excuse to procrastinate on studying was welcome. In the midst of the scripted hullaballoo on screen one evening, the characters enjoyed a Dutch baby pancake—a sweet, popover-like . . . well, pancake. It is simple and comes together quickly in a bowl (or in a blender, if you don't mind noise in the morning). The batter isn't sweet, so if you prefer a sweet pancake, add as much sugar as you'd like to the ingredients; I think 3 Tbsp should be sufficient to please any sweet tooth. It's fantastic served as a normal pancake, with a dotting of butter and a thick lacing of amber maple syrup. Or try it with butter and jam, or eat it like a crêpe, with wedges of lemon and a dusting of confectioners' sugar.**

**3 large eggs, at room temperature**
**¼ tsp fine-grain sea salt**
**½ cup/120 ml milk, at room temperature**
**1½ tsp pure vanilla extract**
**½ cup/60 g all-purpose flour**
**Heaping 1 Tbsp granulated sugar**
**2 Tbsp unsalted butter**

Position a rack in the center of the oven. Preheat the oven to 425°F/220°C. Put a large cast-iron skillet in the oven.

In a large bowl, whisk together the eggs and salt until they're light in color. Whisk in the milk and vanilla. Vigorously whisk in the flour and sugar until all lumps are gone, about 20 seconds.

Carefully remove the cast-iron skillet from the oven. (Remember to put an oven mitt on before handling the hot pan—I've forgotten to do so, and it's very painful!) Add the butter to the pan. Allow the butter to melt, and cajole it around and up the sides of the pan with a pastry brush (I prefer to use a heat-resistant silicone pastry brush to do this).

Pour the batter into the hot pan and return the pan to the oven.

Bake for 20 to 25 minutes, until the center is set and the edges are puffed and a lovely light golden brown.

Using a silicone spatula, remove the Dutch Baby from the pan and transfer it to a wire rack for 3 minutes. Immediately slice it up and dole it out.

### notes

For a quicker method, get out a blender to mix the batter; however, as I've mentioned in other recipes, I always find an excuse to avoid the clamor of powerful kitchen machinery early in the morning. If you do get lumps in your batter with the mixing method explained in this recipe, simply run everything through a sieve—lumps begone!

You don't need a cast-iron skillet to make this recipe. You can simply use a 9-in/23-cm cake pan or a skillet with an ovenproof handle. If you're using a cake pan, put it on a rimmed baking sheet to make transporting it in and out of the oven easy.

# CINNAMON-RAISIN GRANOLA

**MAKES ABOUT 4 CUPS/460 G**

**I don't count calories or deny myself delicious foods, but I do like to eat healthfully. I adore a warm pastry early in the morning, but on days where I haven't the time, the patience, or the desire to bake something, this granola does me good. It's a bit hippie-like in its content: It includes coconut oil, applesauce, and honey. But I love that (and I think you will, too). It is a step up from a bowl of boring sugar-filled cereal, and much more satisfying. I like to mix thin slices of banana into this granola, top it with a big dollop of plain yogurt, and drizzle it with honey.**

**3 cups/465 g rolled oats (not quick-cooking)**

**1¼ cups/210 g raisins**

**⅔ cup/65 g sweetened shredded coconut (optional)**

**⅓ cup/75 ml smooth applesauce, lightly sweetened or unsweetened**

**⅓ cup/70 g coconut oil, melted (see Note)**

**⅓ cup/115 g honey**

**1 Tbsp ground cinnamon**

**¼ tsp fine-grain sea salt**

Position a rack in the center of the oven. Preheat the oven to 250°F/120°C.

In a large mixing bowl, toss together the oats, raisins, and shredded coconut (if using). In a separate bowl or large measuring cup, whisk together the applesauce, coconut oil, honey, cinnamon, and salt. Pour the applesauce mixture into the oat mixture and mix thoroughly.

Spread the granola evenly on a rimmed baking sheet. Bake for 60 to 75 minutes, until it is fragrant and golden brown, stirring it every 20 minutes or so. Allow the granola to cool completely, and store it in an airtight container for up to 2 weeks.

## notes

Make it ahead: I like to make this granola a little over an hour before I go to bed. That way, all I need to do is take the granola out of the oven when the timer goes off, let it cool on the pan overnight, and enjoy it for breakfast the next morning. Effortless pleasure!

I call for coconut oil in the recipe. I like to use unrefined, natural, virgin coconut oil. It smells and tastes like coconut (some coconut oil doesn't) and is solid at room temperature, so melt it in a small saucepan over low heat after you measure out a leveled ⅓ cup/70 g. If you prefer not to use coconut oil, use any flavorless oil of your choice.

# as easy as 1-2-3

Pie and pastry making seems like a rigid, demanding task, but in reality, things are relaxed and far from demanding. In this section, for example, I encourage you to make your own practically foolproof pie dough to create simple, delicious, out-of-this-world pies that bring back nostalgic memories of childhood summers. I don't expect you'll make pies that turn out like those pictured on magazine covers. You will, however, learn to create a flavorful, butter-filled crust that puffs up in the oven and is a perfect companion for its filling, whether it's a Blue Teeth Blueberry Pie (page 59) or Sarah's Apple Pie (page 55).

There is no big secret to making good pastry, but there are a couple of rules that help you to avoid making a miserable mess: Chill your ingredients, and don't overwork the dough. Follow these guidelines and your crust will turn out beautifully. When the weather is hot, pastry is a bit difficult to handle, so work in a cool area to prevent the butter in the dough from melting. If you have naturally hot hands, quickly soak them in ice water or under cold running tap water to cool them down and make working with pastry a cinch.

# FOOLPROOF PIE DOUGH

**MAKES ONE 9-IN/23-CM DOUBLE-CRUST PIE OR TWO 9- OR 10-IN/23- OR 25-CM TARTS**

**Pie dough is not simply a container for delicious fillings. It has its own star qualities, such as being butter-rich, flaky, flavorful, and tender. This recipe makes my go-to pie dough. You can use it for both savory and sweet pies or tarts (in savory recipes, simply leave out the confectioners' sugar). I usually make a double batch—if I'm taking the trouble to make dough for one pie, I might as well make enough dough to bake another pie whenever I choose. Plus, it freezes beautifully and keeps for a good month or two. This dough comes together using a classical French smearing technique called fraisage, which I picked up from a friend of my uncle's, a French pastry chef, several years ago.**

**2 cups plus heaping 1 Tbsp/250 g all-purpose flour**

**½ cup/50 g confectioners' sugar**

**½ tsp fine-grain sea salt**

**1 cup/225 g cold unsalted butter, cut into approximately ½-in/12-mm cubes**

**⅓ cup/75 ml milk, very cold**

**1 egg yolk, cold**

***To make the dough by hand:***

In a large bowl, whisk together the flour, confectioners' sugar, and salt. Toss in the butter. Use your fingertips to quickly rub together the butter and flour mixture until the butter pieces are the size of chickpeas.

In a glass measuring cup, mix together the milk and egg yolk and add them to the flour mixture all at once. Mix briefly.

***To make the dough in a food processor:***

In the bowl of a food processor, briefly pulse together the flour, confectioners' sugar, and salt. Add the butter and pulse until the butter pieces are the size of chickpeas.

In a glass measuring cup, mix together the milk and egg yolk and add them to the flour mixture all at once. Give the mixture a quick pulse.

Drop the shaggy mass of dough onto a clean work surface. Use the palms of your hands to smear the butter and flour in the dough from one end of the pile to the other. Repeat this until a somewhat structured dough forms.

Divide the dough in half. Form each half into a disk and cover it well in plastic wrap. Refrigerate the disks for at least 2 hours, or overnight. The dough can be refrigerated for up to 3 days or frozen for up to 2 months (wrap it well in plastic wrap and put it in a freezer-safe bag).

continued

## note

After you're prepared and refrigerated the dough, roll it out with a rolling pin (if you don't have one, a wine bottle works) on a clean, lightly floured work surface or between two sheets of parchment paper. I like to dust the parchment and the top of the dough very lightly with flour as a precaution. If you're rolling it out on a floured surface, give the dough a full rotation every now and again to prevent it from sticking. If it does stick, carefully loosen a corner of the dough with a dough scraper or a flexible cake spatula, toss a little flour underneath, and move the spatula around to free it. If the dough tears, just press both sides of the tear together. If the dough tears a lot, brush off the excess flour and pat the dough into a disk. Cover the disk in plastic wrap and put it back in the refrigerator for about 30 minutes. Proceed to roll it out again.

# SARAH'S APPLE PIE

MAKES ONE 9-IN/23-CM DOUBLE-CRUST PIE

**I once read that it's essential to speak to your best friend or someone you are involved with for at least five minutes a day—even if it's mundane talk. Sarah and I have been best friends since middle school; if my poor math skills are correct, that's almost half of my life. Sarah and I are inseparable, and we make it a point to speak to each other for several minutes at least once a day. More often than not, our conversations end with us endearingly insulting each other, but that's just what happens: Everything turns into the real-life version of *Will & Grace* or *The Golden Girls*. We sometimes bake together, too. This pie was one of the first things I taught Sarah how to make.**

**1 recipe Foolproof Pie Dough (page 52)**

## APPLE FILLING

**1 Tbsp strained fresh lemon juice**

**7 apples; 3 sweet and 4 tart (about 1½ lb/680 g; see Note)**

**¼ cup/60 g natural cane sugar or granulated sugar**

**2 Tbsp/30 g packed light muscovado sugar or dark brown sugar**

**⅓ cup/40 g all-purpose flour**

**¾ tsp ground cinnamon**

**½ tsp fine-grain sea salt**

**Pinch of grated nutmeg**

**2 Tbsp unsalted butter, cut into pea-size cubes**

**1 large egg**

**½ tsp natural cane sugar or granulated sugar, plus 1 Tbsp**

**Pinch of fine-grain sea salt**

On a well-floured surface, roll out one disk of dough (keep the other refrigerated) into a ⅛-in-/4-mm-thick circle, about 12 in/30 cm in diameter. Center the dough circle in a 9-in/23-cm pie pan and trim the edges, leaving a ½-in/12-mm overhang. Put it in the freezer to chill for 10 minutes.

TO MAKE THE FILLING: Pour the lemon juice into a large mixing bowl. Peel, core, and cut the apples one at a time into ⅓-in/¾-cm slices, tossing them in the lemon juice as you add them to the bowl (this will prevent the apples from browning).

Add the cane sugar, muscovado sugar, flour, cinnamon, salt, and nutmeg to the apples. Carefully toss the mixture together.

Put the filling in the dough-lined pie pan. Evenly dot with the butter.

Roll out the second disk of pie dough into a ⅛-in-/4-mm-thick circle, about 12 in/30 cm in diameter. Put the dough circle over the filling and trim the edges, leaving a ½-in/12-mm overhang. Tuck the top crust edges under the bottom crust, rolling it under all around the pan. Pinch the crusts together to close them, and crimp the edges of the crust with your fingers or press them down with a fork.

Put the pie in the freezer for 15 minutes, making sure it sits flat so nothing will spill out.

While the pie is chilling, position two racks in the center and lower third of the oven. Preheat the oven to 350°F/180°C.

continued

In a small bowl, whisk together the egg, ½ tsp cane sugar, and salt.

Take the pie out of the freezer. Carefully cut four or five slits in the center of the top crust to allow steam to escape while the pie is baking. Lightly and evenly brush the egg mixture on the crust, making sure that the egg does not pool anywhere. Sprinkle the top of the pie evenly with the remaining 1 Tbsp cane sugar; you probably won't need the entire amount.

Put a foil-lined rimmed baking sheet on the lower rack to catch any juices overflowing from the pie as it bakes. Put the pie on the center rack and bake for 1 hour and 15 minutes. After 40 minutes, check to see if the crust is starting to brown, even though the rest of the pie hasn't had enough time in the oven. If it is, carefully place strips of foil around the crust edges to prevent burning or over-browning. When it is done, the pie should be golden brown and the filling should be bubbling and thick.

Transfer the pie to a wire rack and let it cool for at least 1 hour before serving.

## notes

Sweet or tart? I like to use a combination of Granny Smith (tart) and Rome (sweet) apples for this pie—but it's fine to use any equivalent baking apples.

If you want to top the pie with a lattice crust, roll out the chilled second disk of pie dough and cut it into ¾-in/2-cm strips. Lay half the strips of dough across the filling in one direction, and the other half in the other direction, carefully weaving them in and out of one another to create a basket pattern.

As in many of the recipes in this book, I think it's essential to serve this pie warm and topped with vanilla bean ice cream. Warm apple pie à la mode is something that's cherished by all.

# BLUE TEETH BLUEBERRY PIE

MAKES ONE 9-IN/23-CM DOUBLE-CRUST PIE

**This pie hits the nail directly on the head. Its crust is curiously flaky, flavorful, and tender, and its filling is well balanced. It brings back memories of a flawless childhood summer during which I ate my first blueberry pie at a small neighborhood family bakery that was closing its doors that very same day. The moment I bit into that pie, I felt my spirit doing cartwheels and flips—I'd never tasted such perfection. I smiled and my sister laughed, exclaiming, "You have blue teeth!" After I'd spent several summers dreaming about that blueberry pie, I ran into the kitchen and created my own version.**

**Standard ingredients go into the filling for this pie: sugar, flour to hold the berries together, a knifepoint of cinnamon, a pinch of salt, and a scattering of pea-size bits of butter to heighten the flavor of the berries. When you take this pie out of the oven, its top crust is a beautiful walnut-brown, the juices are bubbling away, and small ribbons of steam are fluttering through the pie vents. It's truly a picture-perfect moment.**

**1 recipe Foolproof Pie Dough (page 52)**

## BLUEBERRY FILLING

**½ cup/100 g natural cane sugar or granulated sugar**

**2 Tbsp packed light muscovado sugar or dark brown sugar**

**3 Tbsp all-purpose flour**

**¾ tsp fine-grain sea salt**

**¼ tsp ground cinnamon**

**4 cups/600 g fresh blueberries, washed and dried**

**2 Tbsp unsalted butter, cut into pea-size cubes**

**1 large egg**

**1 Tbsp natural cane sugar or granulated sugar**

On a well-floured surface, roll out one disk of dough (keep the other refrigerated) into a ⅛-in-/4-mm-thick circle, about 12 in/30 cm in diameter. Center the dough circle in a 9-in/23-cm pie pan and trim the edges, leaving a ½-in/12-mm overhang. Put it in the freezer to chill for 10 minutes.

TO MAKE THE FILLING: In a large bowl, whisk together the ½ cup/100 g cane sugar, muscovado sugar, flour, salt, and cinnamon until there are no lumps. Toss in the blueberries, and coat them well.

Put the filling in the dough-lined pie pan. Evenly dot with the butter.

Roll out the second disk of pie dough into a ⅛-in-/4-mm-thick circle, about 12 in/30 cm in diameter. Put the dough circle over the filling and trim the edges, leaving a ½-in/12-mm overhang. Tuck the top crust edges under the bottom crust, rolling it under all around the pan. Pinch the crusts together to close them, and crimp the edges of the crust with your fingers or press them down with a fork.

*continued*

Put the pie in the freezer for 15 minutes, making sure it sits flat so nothing will spill out.

While the pie is chilling, position two racks in the center and lower third of the oven. Preheat the oven to 425°F/220°C.

In a small bowl, whisk together the egg and ½ tsp of the cane sugar.

Take the pie out of the freezer. Carefully cut four or five slits in the center of the top crust to allow steam to escape while the pie is baking. Lightly and evenly brush the egg mixture on the crust, making sure that the egg does not pool anywhere. Sprinkle the top of the pie evenly with the remaining cane sugar; you probably won't need the entire amount.

Put a foil-lined rimmed baking sheet on the lower rack to catch any juices overflowing from the pie as it bakes. Put the pie on the center rack and bake for 20 minutes, after which I usually find that the crust is starting to brown, even though the rest of the pie hasn't had enough time in the oven. If it is, carefully place strips of foil around the crust edges to prevent burning or over-browning. Lower the heat to 350°F/180°C and continue baking for an additional 22 to 30 minutes, until the pie is golden brown and the filling is bubbling and thick.

Transfer the pie to a wire rack to cool for at least 1 hour before serving. I usually let it cool completely so that the filling will thicken further and blueberry juices will not run everywhere once I cut the pie.

### note

Blueberries freeze well. They are at their peak in the summer; if you can, stock up on them during this time and freeze them.

# CHOCOLATE PUDDING PIE

**MAKES ONE 9-IN/23-CM SINGLE-CRUST PIE**

**This is a chocolate lover's dream wrapped in a gorgeous, golden-kissed, buttery pie crust. Your friends and family will constantly find excuses to have you bake it for them, so this is one of the recipes everyone needs in their baking arsenal. The filling has an exemplary balance of chocolate and sweetness, and once baked, the pie transforms into fudgy, pudding-y, brownie-like heaven.**

**½ recipe Foolproof Pie Dough (page 52)**

## CHOCOLATE FILLING

**3½ oz/100 g bittersweet dark chocolate (70 percent cacao), roughly chopped**

**1¼ cups/250 g natural cane sugar or granulated sugar**

**2 large eggs**

**2 tsp pure vanilla extract**

**¼ tsp fine-grain sea salt**

**¾ cup/180 ml heavy (whipping) cream, heated to slightly warmer than body temperature**

**Billowy Whipped Cream (page 65) or vanilla bean ice cream for serving**

Position a rack in the center of the oven. Preheat the oven to 350°F/180°C.

On a well-floured surface, roll out the disk of dough into a ⅛-in-/4-mm-thick circle, about 12 in/30 cm in diameter. Center the dough in a 9-in/23-cm pie pan and trim the edges, leaving a ½-in/12-mm overhang. Fold the overhanging dough under the rim of the pan, and crimp the edges of the crust with your fingers or a fork. Put the crust in the freezer to chill for 10 minutes. Remove the crust from the freezer and poke the bottom of the crust all over with a fork. Line the crust with foil or crumpled parchment paper, and fill it with pie weights (see Note) until they reach the top edge of the crust.

Bake for about 15 minutes. Remove the foil and weights and bake for about 10 minutes more, until the crust appears dry but not browned. Allow the crust to cool while you make the filling. Leave the oven on.

**TO MAKE THE FILLING:** Melt the chocolate in a large, heatproof bowl set over a saucepan of simmering water. (Or put it in the microwave on a low setting for about 1 minute, stirring every 20 seconds until it is completely melted.) Whisk the sugar, eggs, vanilla, and salt into the chocolate. The mixture will appear gritty. Stir in the cream and mix well until the entire mixture is smooth.

Pour the filling into the pie shell and put the pie pan on the rimmed baking sheet. Bake for 42 to 47 minutes, until the filling is light in color and crackly on top and the center is slightly jiggly. Be sure to check the pie halfway through baking; if the crust is browning significantly (which can happen if you've put the pie pan on a dark-colored baking sheet), carefully cover the crust with strips of foil.

*continued*

Once the pie is baked, transfer it to a wire rack and allow it to cool completely before cutting it into wedges. Serve with a big dollop of whipped cream.

### note

What are pie weights? They are weighted objects used to prevent pie dough from puffing up and drooping down the sides of the pan as it prebakes. Pie weights come in various forms; some are small ceramic or stainless-steel spheres, while others are small chains. Pie weights, despite their name, don't have to weigh a lot to be effective, and you don't even have to buy the expensive ceramic spheres made especially for pie baking—dried beans, rice, or pennies work just as well. Of course, you can't eat the beans or rice after you use them as pie weights, but do save them to use in baking other crusts.

# BILLOWY WHIPPED CREAM

**MAKES ABOUT 2 CUPS/480 ML**

**The mixing method for this whipped cream is somewhat unusual, but it results in a beautifully droopy and billowy topping that's perfect for adorning pastries and cakes. I usually whip the cream by hand in a large bowl with a whisk—it's a good workout. However, a handheld mixer or stand mixer works just as well. Feel free to adjust the sugar to suit your taste.**

- **1 cup/240 ml heavy (whipping) cream**
- **2 Tbsp confectioners' sugar**
- **1 tsp pure vanilla extract (optional)**

Put a large bowl in the freezer to chill for several minutes before beginning.

In the chilled bowl, using a balloon whisk or a handheld mixer (or in the bowl of a stand mixer fitted with the whisk attachment), whip together ½ cup/120 ml of the cream and the confectioners' sugar until firm, stiff peaks form. Whisk in the vanilla (if using). Lightly whisk in the remaining cream to create an ethereal whipped cream.

Keep the whipped cream refrigerated, covered with plastic wrap, for up to 2 hours before using.

## notes

Though I've gotten away with storing whipped cream in the refrigerator for a couple of days, I notice that the mixture gets a bit stiff and needs a bit of cream stirred in until it's back to being billowy again. If you plan to store whipped cream for more than a day, put it in a sealed, odorless container in the refrigerator so it doesn't absorb other flavorings.

You'll find different types of cream depending on where you live: heavy cream, light or heavy whipping cream, or, if you're in the United Kingdom, double cream. Heavy cream has around 40 percent fat content and isn't available everywhere in the United States; however, light and heavy whipping creams are available and are sometimes simply called whipping cream. The latter two types have 30 and 40 percent fat content, respectively. Because both types of cream are meant for whipping, they usually contain stabilizers and gums to help thicken the cream and prevent it from curdling. Double cream has around 48 percent fat content, making it thicker than the other types of cream. It's readily available throughout the United Kingdom.

## variations

Whipped cream is a very versatile creature and can be enhanced in any way that you'd like. Experiment with the use of other extracts (or varieties of alcohol) besides vanilla.

You can fold roughly chopped pistachios or other sorts of nuts into the whipped cream; sweeten it with honey, golden syrup, or maple syrup; or leave it unsweetened, with only the kiss of vanilla or other flavoring.

For a chocolatey whipped cream, simply stir in up to 2 Tbsp sifted unsweetened cocoa powder (natural or Dutch-processed) along with the vanilla.

# MAPLE-PECAN PIE

**MAKES ONE 9-IN/23-CM SINGLE-CRUST PIE**

**I made this pie out of necessity on Thanksgiving a couple of years ago. My cupboard was almost bare (hard to believe about an obsessive baker like me!) after a midnight stint of failed baking attempts. I had only a packet of pecans and a huge jug of pure maple syrup. Instantly I thought, "Pecan pie with maple syrup!" The deliciously smooth and silken maple syrup adds much more depth of flavor and richness to the pie than golden syrup or light corn syrup could; it is truly remarkable.**

**½ recipe Foolproof Pie Dough (page 52)**

## MAPLE-PECAN FILLING

**½ cup/100 g packed light brown sugar**

**¼ cup/55 g unsalted butter, melted**

**½ tsp fine-grain sea salt**

**1 cup/240 ml pure maple syrup (see Note)**

**3 large eggs plus 1 egg yolk, at room temperature**

**1 Tbsp pure vanilla extract**

**2 cups/260 g roughly chopped toasted pecans**

**Billowy Whipped Cream (page 65) for serving**

Position a rack in the center of the oven. Preheat the oven to 350°F/180°C.

On a well-floured surface, roll out the disk of dough into a ⅛-in-/4-mm-thick circle, about 12 in/30 cm in diameter. Center the dough in a 9-in/23-cm pie pan and trim the edges, leaving a ½-in/12-mm overhang. Fold the overhanging dough under the rim of the pan, and crimp the edges of the crust with your fingers or a fork. Put the crust in the freezer to chill for 10 minutes.

Remove the crust from the freezer and lightly poke the bottom of the crust all over with a fork. Line the crust with foil or crumpled parchment paper, and fill with pie weights (see Note, page 64) until they reach the top edge of the crust.

Bake for about 15 minutes. Remove the foil and weights and bake for about 10 minutes more, until the crust appears dry but not browned. Allow the crust to cool while you make the filling.

**TO MAKE THE FILLING:** In a large bowl, whisk together the brown sugar, butter, and salt until there are no lumps. Whisk in the maple syrup, eggs, egg yolk, and vanilla until well combined. Stir in the pecans. Pour the filling into the pie shell and put the pie pan on a rimmed baking sheet. Bake for 50 to 60 minutes, until the center of the filling is set yet slightly jiggly. Be sure to check the pie halfway through baking; if the crust is browning significantly (which can happen if you've put the pie pan on a dark-colored baking sheet), carefully cover the crust with strips of foil.

Once the pie is baked, transfer it to a wire rack to cool completely before cutting it into wedges. Serve with a big dollop of whipped cream.

### *note*

Pancake syrup and pure maple syrup are two very different things, and the former won't work well in this recipe. But if you don't want a maple-flavored pie, or if you simply have trouble finding pure maple syrup (especially true for my European friends), you can substitute golden syrup or even light corn syrup one for one for the maple syrup.

# VERY BEST PUMPKIN PIE

**MAKES ONE 10-IN/25-CM SINGLE-CRUST PIE**

**I am very finicky when it comes to pies—especially pumpkin pie. It's the thing I crave on an almost-daily basis once autumn rolls around. First and foremost, a good crust-to-filling ratio is essential. Second, the pie must have a nice balance of warm spices in its custardy filling—in this case, cinnamon, ginger, nutmeg, and cloves. The spices mustn't be overpowering, and there should be discernible pumpkin flavor.**

**½ recipe Foolproof Pie Dough (page 52)**

## PUMPKIN FILLING

**¾ cup/150 g packed light muscovado sugar or brown sugar**

**¼ cup/50 g natural cane sugar**

**1½ tsp ground cinnamon**

**1½ tsp ground ginger**

**¾ tsp fine-grain sea salt**

**¼ tsp ground nutmeg**

**⅛ tsp ground cloves**

**One 15-oz/425-g can pure pumpkin purée (not pumpkin pie filling)**

**1½ cups/375 ml heavy (whipping) cream, at room temperature**

**3 large eggs plus 1 egg yolk, at room temperature**

**Billowy Whipped Cream (page 65) for serving**

Position a rack in the center of the oven. Preheat the oven to 425°F/220°C.

On a well-floured surface, roll out the disk of dough into a ⅛-in-/4-mm-thick circle, about 12 in/30 cm in diameter. Fit the dough into the bottom and sides of a 10-by-1-in/25-by-2.5-cm loose-bottom tart pan. Trim the excess dough flush with the rim of the pan, using a knife or a large rolling pin rolled over the top of the pan. Put the crust in the freezer to chill for about 25 minutes, until firm.

**TO MAKE THE FILLING:** In a large bowl, whisk together the muscovado sugar, cane sugar, cinnamon, ginger, salt, nutmeg, and cloves. Whisk in the pumpkin purée, followed by the cream, eggs, and egg yolk. Whisk well, making sure there aren't any lumps in the mixture.

Put the tart pan on a rimmed baking sheet. Pour the pumpkin filling into the tart shell (there might be some left over, freeze in a resealable bag for up to 2 months; simply defrost and whisk until smooth), being sure to leave about ⅓ in/8 mm of space between the top of the filling and the top edge of the crust (the filling will puff up a bit during baking). Bake for 10 minutes, lower the heat to 350°F/180°C, and continue baking for 30 minutes more, until the filling is puffy and the center is just set.

Transfer the pie to a wire rack to cool for about 2 hours. Remove the side of the tart pan before slicing the pie, and serve each piece topped with a big dollop of whipped cream.

### *note*

When it comes to pumpkin pie, I like to have more filling than crust on my fork—one reason I use a tart shell. Another reason is that I don't have the patience to crimp pie dough, and a tart pan takes that headache away. I call for a 10-by-1-in/25-by-2.5-cm loose-bottom tart pan for this recipe. However, you can make this in a 9-in/23-cm pie pan, too. Follow the recipe, and bake the pie for 52 to 60 minutes, until the filling is puffy and the center is just set.

# EASY MEYER LEMON TART

**MAKES ONE 10-IN/25-CM TART**

**This is not exactly your conventional lemon tart. Often, lemon tart recipes ask you to cook a custard filling in a tart pan, which results in a mess and often yields a soggy-bottomed crust—a no-no. So I prebake a tart shell, fill it up with lemon curd, and allow the curd to set in a hot oven for a few minutes. Then I adorn the top with fresh berries and a dusting of confectioners' sugar. That's it.**

**I like to prepare a Meyer lemon curd whenever I can get my hands on the sweet, mandarin orange–flavored fruit. But ordinary lemons work well, too. If you're short on time or don't have the patience to make your own lemon curd (it happens to all of us), a good-quality store-bought lemon curd will do. Just make sure you have enough to fill the tart (about 1½ cups/500 g).**

**½ recipe Foolproof Pie Dough (page 52)**

## MEYER LEMON CURD

**2 tsp Meyer lemon zest**

**6 Tbsp/90 ml fresh Meyer lemon juice**

**¼ cup/50 g granulated sugar**

**3 large eggs plus 1 egg yolk**

**Pinch of fine-grain sea salt**

**7 Tbsp/100 g unsalted butter, cut into ½-in/12-mm cubes**

Position a rack in the center of the oven. Preheat the oven to 400°F/200°C.

On a well-floured surface, roll out the disk of dough into a ⅛-in-/4-mm-thick circle, about 12 in/30 cm in diameter. Fit the dough into the bottom and sides of a 10-by-1-in/25-by-2.5-cm loose-bottom tart pan. Trim the excess dough flush with the rim of the pan, using a knife or a large rolling pin rolled over the top of the pan. Put the crust in the freezer to chill for about 25 minutes, until firm.

Remove the crust from the freezer and poke the bottom of the crust all over with a fork. Line the crust with foil or crumpled parchment paper, and fill with pie weights (see Note, page 64) until they reach the top edge of the crust.

Bake for about 15 minutes. Remove the foil and weights and bake for about 10 minutes more, until the crust appears dry and golden brown. Allow the crust to cool while you make the lemon curd. Leave the oven on.

**TO MAKE THE LEMON CURD:** In a medium saucepan over low heat, whisk together the lemon zest, lemon juice, sugar, eggs, egg yolk, and salt. Add the butter, continuously whisking the mixture until the butter is melted. Keep whisking the mixture until it thickens and becomes as viscous as honey. It's done when a figure-eight briefly holds on the surface of the lemon curd when whisking.

Put the tart pan on a rimmed baking sheet. Push the cooked curd through a sieve and into the tart shell. Bake for 4 to 7 minutes, until the curd is set.

Transfer the tart to a wire rack to cool completely. Remove the side of the tart pan before slicing the tart and serving.

## notes

You can prepare and bake the tart shell up to 1 day in advance, and then make the curd and fill the tart when you want to bake it. The curd can be prepared up to 1 week before you make the tart.

The curd doesn't need to completely set in the oven—but if it does, slicing the tart will be less messy (the tart in the photo is just set, so it is still a bit custardy when sliced, which I like a lot).

## variation

If you don't have access to Meyer lemons, use regular lemons; simply increase the amount of sugar called for in the curd to ½ cup/100 g.

# MILLE-FEUILLES

**SERVES 4 OR 5**

**My late grandfather was a big fan of mille-feuilles (also known as napoleons). The version he loved came from a tiny Russian bakery in Queens. A sweet little babushka made the pastry once a week, and the minute the huge pans of napoleons left the small kitchen in back, people from around the neighborhood lined up outside the small store to buy the grandmother's pastries. This version is not as involved as the mille-feuilles of my childhood; the classic version involves layering thin sheets of baked pastry with lightly sweetened pastry cream. This recipe skips that laborious process and provides near-instant gratification by layering Billowy Whipped Cream and fruit (passion fruit here) between a couple sheets of thin puff pastry. Simple enough, right?**

- **1 cup/100 g confectioners' sugar**
- **½ recipe Quick Puff Pastry (page 37) or 8 oz/225 g store-bought puff pastry**
- **½ recipe Billowy Whipped Cream (page 65)**
- **1 ripe passion fruit, cut in half and seeds scraped out (see Variations for alternatives)**

Position a rack in the upper third of the oven. Preheat the oven to 400°F/200°C. Line a rimmed baking sheet with parchment paper and set it aside.

Sprinkle a clean work surface with ½ cup/50 g of the confectioners' sugar, put the puff pastry dough on the work surface, and dust its top with more sugar. Roll the dough into an 8-by-11-in/ 20-by-28-cm rectangle. Trim the edges with a sharp knife to straighten everything out, and cut the rectangle in half so you have two 8-by-5½-in/ 20-by-14-cm pieces of dough. Transfer them to the parchment-lined baking sheet and put it in the freezer for 15 minutes until firm.

Remove it from the freezer and prick both halves of the dough all over with a fork. Bake for 12 minutes. Remove the pan from the oven and carefully press a clean kitchen towel on the pastry to get out all the air. Sprinkle the top of each pastry half with more sugar.

Return the pan to the oven and bake for 12 to 15 minutes more, until the pastry is bronzed and flaky. Allow the pastry to cool completely.

Dust the top of each half with more sugar. Using an offset spatula or the back of an ordinary tablespoon, spread half of the whipped cream onto one of the pastry halves. Top with half of the passion fruit, place the other pastry half on top of the fruit (you're going for a sandwich effect here), spread the remaining whipped cream on top of that, and decorate the top with the remaining fruit. Using a sharp serrated knife, cut the pastry into four or five pieces and serve.

## variations

Be creative: You can put whatever sliced fruit you want between the layers of pastry, and then top the pastry with more fruit. Strawberries, raspberries, blueberries, blackberries, kiwi, or mango—or a combination thereof—work well. Another great variation is to use slices of ripe mango and strawberries between the layers of baked pastry and then top the pastry with wedged strawberries, sliced passion fruit, and a smattering of pistachio nuts.

# ARABIAN NIGHTS BAKLAVA

**MAKES MORE THAN 100 PIECES**

**Baklava is a sweet, rich pastry layered with brushstrokes of clarified butter and smatterings of spiced nuts (here walnuts and pistachios). The pastry is cut into diamond shapes before it visits a warm oven, then the pastry diamonds are covered with a sweet, orange-infused honey syrup. The pastry's exact origin is unknown; many ethnic groups claim to be the creators of this rich dessert. It's also said to have been a food preferred by the Arabian wealthy, and understandably so, as baklava is somewhat expensive and tedious to make. However, the repetitive efforts of layering pastry and brushing on butter are well worth it—an Arabian night can be enjoyed with a group of your favorite people and several pieces of this beautiful, sensuous pastry.**

## ORANGE-HONEY SYRUP

**2/3 cup/135 g granulated sugar**

**Juice of 1 medium orange; reserve the orange halves**

**3/4 cup/255 g honey**

## PASTRY AND FILLING

**1 lb/455 g phyllo pastry sheets**

**1 cup/240 ml Clarified Butter (page 79) or 3/4 cup/180 ml prepared ghee**

**2 cups/225 g whole walnuts**

**1 cup/115 g unsalted pistachios, plus more roughly chopped for garnish**

**1/3 cup/65 g granulated sugar**

**Scant 1 Tbsp ground cinnamon**

**TO MAKE THE SYRUP:** In a medium saucepan, stir together the sugar, orange juice, and 3/4 cup/180 ml water.

Add the juiced orange halves. Set the pan over medium heat and bring the mixture to a boil, stirring often until the sugar has dissolved. Stir in the honey and turn the heat to medium-low. Let the mixture simmer for 7 to 10 minutes, until it's slightly thickened. Pour the hot syrup through a sieve into a heatproof bowl. Be sure to press firmly on the solids in the sieve to get out any excess syrup, then discard the solids. Allow the strained syrup to cool for 30 minutes at room temperature before transferring the bowl to the refrigerator to cool completely.

**TO MAKE THE PASTRY AND FILLING:** Position a rack in the center of the oven. Preheat the oven to 350°F/180°C. Generously butter the bottom and sides of a 9-by-13-in/23-by-33-cm baking pan. Set aside.

Cut the phyllo to fit the pan snugly, and cover the stack of phyllo with a damp dish towel so it won't dry out as you work. Lay one sheet of phyllo in the pan and brush clarified butter onto it. Add a second sheet of phyllo and brush it with more butter. Repeat the process with six more sheets of phyllo.

To give the nut filling an ideal texture, pulse about half of the walnuts and pistachios with the sugar and cinnamon in a food processor, until they've turned into coarse crumbs. Pulse in the rest of the nuts (a couple of pulses should do) so that there is some texture in the filling. (You don't have to be too scientific; simply chopping everything with a knife works well, too.) Sprinkle a thin, even layer of the nut filling over the buttered phyllo in the pan.

Layer and butter another four sheets of phyllo and sprinkle a thin layer of the filling atop them. Repeat this step twice. At this point, you should have used twenty sheets of phyllo.

*continued*

Sprinkle the remaining nut mixture on top, and layer and butter another eight sheets of phyllo atop it (for a total of twenty-eight sheets of phyllo).

Brush butter over the top layer, cover the pan with plastic wrap, and transfer it to the refrigerator for 10 minutes to allow the butter to firm up slightly (this will facilitate the cutting process).

Remove the pan from the refrigerator. Using a sharp knife, carefully cut the layered phyllo diagonally into 1½-in-/4-cm-wide rectangles. Cut diagonally the other way to make diamond-shaped pieces. Be careful not to shift the phyllo sheets while cutting.

Bake for 45 to 55 minutes, until the pastry is lightly bronzed.

While the baklava is still hot, pour half of the cold syrup evenly over the top. Allow the syrup a few minutes to seep into the pastry, and pour the remaining half of the cold syrup onto the pastry.

Garnish the pastry with roughly chopped pistachios. Set it aside to cool to room temperature before serving, and cover with plastic wrap before storing. (In an ideal world, you should allow baklava to cool and sit for 8 hours or overnight for the flavors to meld, but about 4 hours works if you're impatient.)

The baklava will keep, covered, at room temperature for up to 1 week.

# CLARIFIED BUTTER

**Clarified butter is great for many cooking needs, as it has a high smoke point (meaning it doesn't burn as easily). It's wonderful not only for making baklava, but for omelets as well.**

**MAKES ¾ CUP/175 ML**

**8 oz/225 g unsalted butter**

Line a sieve with a paper towel or coffee filter. If you're using the latter, gently run the filter under hot water for a couple of seconds to get rid of any factory residues and to allow the filter to sit in the sieve better; tap gently to get rid of any excess water. Put the sieve over a bowl.

Cube the butter and put it in a heavy-bottom saucepan over medium heat until it begins to foam. Using a large metal spoon, skim the foam off the top of the butter and discard.

Remove the pan from the heat and pour the butter into the lined sieve, which will strain out the milk solids. Discard the milk solids left in the sieve, or put them in a bowl, refrigerate, and use on pancakes.

Clarified butter will keep in an airtight container at room temperature for up to 1 month.

# Three o'clock

"Think what a better world it would be if we all, the whole world, had cookies and milk about three o'clock every afternoon and then lay down on our blankets for a nap."

—Barbara Jordan

Cookies, whether they're round or bars, can transform anyone's mood, no matter a person's age. This section will help you console a friend in need, cheer up a loved one after a tough day, and simply put smiles on everyone's faces. I've never seen anyone with furrowed eyebrows, a frown, and a cookie in their hand—indeed, these tiny confections have magical wrinkle-smoothing, smile-inducing capabilities. The cookie recipes that follow are meant to please anyone, and they come in all forms: drop cookies, slice-and-bake dough, and bar cookies such as blondies.

In this section, you'll also find the very best chocolate chip cookie recipe—one that will end your search for the perfect nibble—as well as brownies that are ideal for storing in the freezer and snacking upon on a whim.

Cookies, I feel, are called for on Mondays. Always. On other days, they're called for at three o'clock to help boost any sluggish spirit. A nap afterward is optional but highly recommended.

**STORING COOKIE DOUGH:**

Unless you absolutely want to bake a few dozen cookies in a day, store extra cookie dough in the freezer. First portion out the dough onto a parchment-lined baking sheet, and place the sheet in the freezer for about 30 minutes, or until the dough is firm. Transfer the portioned-out dough to freezer-safe resealable bags marked with the kind of cookie dough and the date. Most cookie doughs freeze safely for up to 6 months.

# SPARKLY SUGAR COOKIES

**MAKES ABOUT 36 COOKIES**

**Beautifully thin, soft sugar cookies covered in a ring of colored sugar: They're every child's—and in my case, inner child's—dream. There is no need for excessive fuss with these cookies. You put everything into one bowl and mix until a dough ball forms. You can also use a food processor—remember to use the pulse function, as you don't want to overmix the cookie dough.**

- **2½ cups/300 g all-purpose flour**
- **¾ cup/150 g granulated sugar**
- **½ tsp baking soda**
- **½ tsp fine-grain sea salt**
- **1 cup/225 g unsalted butter, at room temperature, roughly cubed**
- **2 Tbsp milk or heavy (whipping) cream**
- **2 tsp pure vanilla extract**
- **¼ cup/50 g colored sanding sugar (see Note)**

In a large bowl using a handheld mixer, or in the bowl of a stand mixer fitted with the paddle attachment, mix together the flour, granulated sugar, baking soda, and salt on low speed for about 15 seconds. Add the butter, milk, and vanilla and mix on low speed until a dough ball forms.

Roll the dough into two 9-in/23-cm logs on parchment paper or plastic wrap, twisting the ends shut. Refrigerate the logs for at least 2 hours, or up to 3 days.

Position a rack in the upper third of the oven. Preheat the oven to 350°F/180°C. Line a rimmed baking sheet with parchment paper.

Unwrap the logs, roll them in the colored sanding sugar, and cut them into ½-in-/12-mm-thick rounds. Place the cookies about 2 in/5 cm apart on the prepared baking sheet. Bake for 10 to 12 minutes, until the edges are lightly golden brown.

Allow the cookies to cool for a couple of minutes on the pans before transferring them to a wire rack. The cookies will keep in an airtight container at room temperature for up to 3 days.

## notes

For the pictured cookies, I used vanilla bean paste—I love seeing little flecks of vanilla bean throughout the cookies. If you're interested in going my route, simply substitute vanilla bean paste one to one for the vanilla extract called for in the recipe.

You can make your own colored sanding sugar if you have food coloring on hand. Use about ⅓ cup/65 g cane sugar, turbinado sugar, Demerara sugar, or plain granulated sugar to make your own. Just divide the sugar into small bowls, add a drop or two of food coloring (or the tiniest dab of gel coloring) to each bowl, mix, and . . . voilà! Colored sanding sugar.

## variation

To change things up a bit, use almond extract instead of vanilla extract. Almond extract is a little more powerful than vanilla extract, so I use only 1 tsp of it. Taste the dough after adding the extract, and if you feel it needs more, mix it into the dough in ¼-tsp increments until the flavor is to your liking.

# VERY BEST CHOCOLATE CHIP COOKIES

**MAKES ABOUT 36 COOKIES**

**It's a strong statement to claim that these are simply the very best chocolate chip cookies around, but it does them justice. Everything about these just works. The cookies are in all ways bold, sophisticated, sexy, and luscious. They have tenderly crisp edges, soft centers, and sunrise-hued bottoms—every chocolate chip cookie lover's dream. Because I only ever bake half a batch at a time, I freeze the other half of the dough rounds in a plastic resealable bag (as suggested on page 81) so I can bake cookies during the week.**

- **2 cups/240 g all-purpose flour**
- **3/4 cup/90 g bread flour (see Note)**
- **1 tsp baking soda**
- **3/4 tsp fine-grain sea salt**
- **1/4 tsp baking powder**
- **1 1/4 cups/250 g packed light brown sugar or muscovado sugar**
- **1/2 cup/100 g Demerara or turbinado sugar**
- **1 cup/225 g cold unsalted butter (see Note), cut into rough cubes**
- **1 large egg plus 1 egg yolk**
- **2 Tbsp milk**
- **1 Tbsp vanilla bean paste or pure vanilla extract**
- **10 1/2 oz/300 g dark chocolate (see Note), chopped into chunks**

Line two rimmed baking sheets with parchment paper.

In a medium bowl, whisk together the all-purpose flour, bread flour, baking soda, salt, and baking powder. Set this aside.

Put the brown sugar and Demerara sugar in the bowl of a stand mixer fitted with the paddle attachment (or a large bowl).

In a heavy-bottom medium saucepan over medium heat, warm the butter until it's just melted. Pour it into the bowl of sugar and mix on low speed (use a wooden spoon or a hand-held mixer, if you like) until it's a smooth paste; this will take about 1 minute.

Add the egg, egg yolk, milk, and vanilla bean paste and mix on low speed for another minute, until well combined. Scrape the bowl and test the mixture with your fingers to see if it's at room temperature. If it's even the least bit warm, allow the mixture to cool for a few minutes, as you don't want to melt the chocolate.

With the mixer on low speed, add the flour mixture until just incorporated, about 1 minute. Turn off the mixer and scrape down the sides and bottom of the bowl to make sure all of the flour has been incorporated properly. Stir in the chocolate with a spoon or spatula.

Here's where things get a little unusual; this will allow for layers of chocolate throughout the cookie, instead of one layer of chocolate: Scoop a round, 1-Tbsp portion of dough onto one of the prepared baking sheets. Place another 1-Tbsp portion of dough on top of the first, and lightly press down on the stack of dough just enough to merge them into a single lump about 1 3/4 in/4.5 cm high. Repeat with the rest of the dough, evenly spacing the dough portions about 2 in/5 cm apart (I usually get about nine per sheet).

*continued*

Put the baking sheets in the refrigerator to chill for 30 minutes, or until the dough is firm. About 15 minutes into chilling, position a rack in the center of the oven. Preheat the oven to 375°F/190°C.

Once the dough is chilled, bake one sheet at a time for about 12 minutes, rotating the sheet halfway through baking, until the cookies are lightly golden brown around the edges and their tops are blushed with gold; the cookies will look slightly soft in the center, and almost uncooked, but fear not—they're perfect.

Allow the cookies to cool directly on the baking sheet until it is cool to the touch, 10 to 15 minutes. Transfer the cookies to a wire rack or to your mouth. Repeat with the remaining baking sheet. The cookies will keep in an airtight container at room temperature for up to 3 days.

## notes

The bread flour called for in the recipe is a bit unusual, but the gluten content of the bread flour is what allows these cookies to have such great soft centers; it's definitely a necessity.

If you're using a thin and flimsy baking sheet, double it up with another sheet for protection against the heat of the oven.

Use good-quality butter. If you can, spend a bit extra on a European-style butter; it makes a big difference in the flavor of the final cookies. I highly recommend Kerry Gold, Plugrá, and Smjör.

Use good-quality chocolate, too. Buy the best that you can afford, with 54 to 65 percent cacao. You can either buy bars and use a serrated knife to cut them into chunks or get fancy couverture chocolate online or at specialty shops. Couverture chocolate fèves are basically flat disks. I am partial to Valrhona 64% Manjari fèves, although they are a bit too large for these cookies. I cut each one in half (it's time-consuming, but it makes for an even distribution of chocolate pieces throughout the dough). Or buy E. Guittard's or El Rey's lovely couverture fèves and there'll be no need for chocolate chopping whatsoever because they are smaller in size.

If you have the patience—or laziness—to leave your dough (covered in the mixing bowl) for 36 to 48 hours in the refrigerator before baking, do it. It will allow even more of the caramel flavors within the cookies to come out. Forgetfulness does have its benefits after all.

## variations

If you prefer to use chocolate chips or chocolate chunks instead of regular chocolate, stir in 1¾ cups/300 g of a 12-oz/340-g bag (if you want more chocolate, go ahead and use the whole bag). Using about the same amount of multicolored chocolate candies creates great kid-friendly cookies.

For larger cookies, stack two 4-Tbsp rounds of dough on top of one another and flatten them to about half their original height. Bake about six to a sheet, being sure to leave ample spreading room (about 4 in/10 cm) between the cookies. Larger cookies will take 13 to 15 minutes to bake.

# CHOCOLATE SNICKERDOODLE COOKIES

**MAKES 20 COOKIES**

**When the sweet flavors of chocolate and cinnamon mingle in a soft, slightly cakey cookie, your spirit will feel as if the heavens have wafted right down onto your kitchen counter. The very first time I bit into this cinnamon-sugar-covered, soft chocolate cookie, I blurted out, "Hot dangit!" Because I'm a native New Yorker, it might seem a little unusual to use nonregional expressions, but I don't apologize for that; these cookies are damn good and require enthusiasm, especially when you're practically a member of Chocoholics Anonymous.**

- **2 Tbsp granulated sugar, plus 1½ cups/300 g**
- **2 tsp ground cinnamon**
- **2¼ cups/270 g all-purpose flour**
- **½ cup/50 g unsweetened cocoa powder (natural or Dutch-processed)**
- **2 tsp baking powder**
- **¼ tsp fine-grain sea salt**
- **1 cup/225 g unsalted butter, at room temperature**
- **2 large eggs, at room temperature**
- **1 tsp pure vanilla extract**

Position two racks in the upper third and center of the oven. Preheat the oven to 350°F/180°C. Line two baking sheets with parchment paper.

In a small bowl (preferably a shallow one), mix together the 2 Tbsp sugar and the cinnamon. Set this mixture aside; you'll roll the cookie dough in it later.

In a medium bowl, sift together the flour, cocoa powder, baking powder, and salt. Set this aside.

In a large bowl with a handheld mixer, or in the bowl of a stand mixer fitted with the paddle attachment, whip together the butter and remaining 1½ cups/300 g sugar on medium speed for 3 to 5 minutes, until pale and fluffy. Turn off the mixer and scrape down the sides and bottom of the bowl. On low speed, beat in the eggs and vanilla until well incorporated, about 1 minute. Mix in the flour-cocoa mixture until just combined.

Shape the dough into 3-Tbsp rounds and roll them in the cinnamon-sugar. Place the dough rounds on the prepared baking sheets about 3 in/7.5 cm apart.

Bake the cookies, rotating the baking sheets halfway through, until their edges are set and their middles are soft and shiny, 12 to 15 minutes. Once the cookies are out of the oven, allow them to sit on the baking sheets for 5 minutes, then transfer them to wire racks to cool completely before eating. The cookies will keep in an airtight container at room temperature for up to 3 days.

# HEARTBREAK CHOCOLATE TRUFFLE COOKIES

**MAKES ABOUT 12 COOKIES; ENOUGH FOR A WEEK OR SO OF HEART-MENDING**

**After a heart-wrenching break-up, I found myself making these cookies on a near-daily basis for several weeks; I'd eat one a day, late in the evening, when I felt my soul at its weakest. It was the only way I could get the strong fix of chocolate I needed to mend my aching heart.**

**Chocolate, friendship, and laughter are crucial to mending a broken heart, so make sure to have a couple of these, your best friends on speed dial, and a funny book by your side. And if all else fails, eat cookies and watch videos of cute kittens and puppies on YouTube; all will be well, my dear reader. I promise!**

- **½ cup/115 g unsalted butter, cut into ½-in/12-mm cubes**
- **5 oz/140 g dark chocolate (minimum 64 percent cacao), roughly chopped**
- **⅔ cup/80 g whole-wheat pastry flour**
- **3 Tbsp unsweetened cocoa powder (natural or Dutch-processed)**
- **½ tsp baking powder**
- **½ tsp fine-grain sea salt**
- **¾ cup/150 g packed light brown sugar**
- **2 large eggs**
- **2 tsp pure vanilla extract**
- **1½ cups/340 g chocolate chips or 2¾ cups/350 g shelled unsalted dry-roasted pistachios, or a mixture**

Position a rack in the upper third of the oven. Preheat the oven to 350°F/180°C. Line a rimmed baking sheet with parchment paper.

In the top of a double boiler over simmering water, melt together the butter and dark chocolate. Set aside to cool for a few minutes.

Meanwhile, in a medium bowl, whisk together the flour, cocoa powder, baking powder, and salt and set aside.

In a large bowl with a handheld mixer or in the bowl of a stand mixer fitted with the paddle attachment, beat together the brown sugar, eggs, and vanilla on medium speed until smooth and creamy, about 2 minutes. Turn off the mixer and scrape down the sides and bottom of the bowl. On low speed, beat in the melted butter and chocolate. Turn off the mixer and stir in the flour-cocoa mixture until just combined. Then stir in the chocolate chips.

Drop 3-Tbsp portions of dough onto the prepared baking sheet about 3 in/7.5 cm apart.

Bake for 13 to 16 minutes, rotating the baking sheet halfway through baking, until the cookies are crackly and the centers are still soft. Allow the cookies to cool on the baking sheet for about 10 minutes, or until it is cool to the touch. Then transfer the cookies to a wire rack to cool a bit before eating. The cookies will keep in an airtight container at room temperature for up to 3 days.

### note

During my entire mending period, I never really intended on sharing these cookies (they were for me, after all) with a large crowd of folks, so I found myself, more often than not, baking a couple of these cookies at a time and storing the rest of the cookie dough as per the instructions on page 81.

2013-90-

# TAKE IT AND GO! COOKIES

**MAKES ABOUT 24 COOKIES**

**These cookies aren't your popular, conventionally chewy cookie; instead they're crispy and golden on the outside and ever-so-slightly soft in the center. The dough is flavored with vanilla and almond extracts, but the best part is that these cookies are brimming with milk chocolate chips, white chocolate chips, shredded coconut, and thick shards of macadamia nuts. They definitely qualify as an "everything but the kitchen sink" treat, and when people constantly shadow you in the kitchen until they can grab a cookie off the cooling rack, you'll eventually say, "Oh, just take it and go!"**

- **1 cup/120 g all-purpose flour**
- **¾ cup/90 g whole-wheat pastry flour**
- **½ tsp baking powder**
- **½ tsp fine-grain sea salt**
- **10 Tbsp/140 g unsalted butter, at room temperature**
- **1 cup/200 g packed light brown sugar**
- **¾ cup/150 g granulated sugar**
- **1 large egg, at room temperature**
- **2 tsp pure vanilla extract**
- **¼ tsp pure almond extract**
- **1 cup/170 g milk chocolate chips**
- **1 cup/170 g white chocolate chunks/chips**
- **⅔ cup/75 g dry-roasted unsalted macadamia nuts, roughly chopped**
- **1 cup/120 g lightly packed sweetened shredded coconut (see Note)**

Position two racks in the upper third and center of the oven. Preheat the oven to 325°F/165°C. Line two baking sheets with parchment paper.

In a medium mixing bowl, whisk together the all-purpose flour, pastry flour, baking powder, and salt. Set this aside.

In a large bowl with a handheld mixer or in the bowl of a stand mixer fitted with the paddle attachment, beat together the butter, brown sugar, and granulated sugar on medium speed for 3 to 6 minutes, until pale and creamy. Turn off the mixer and scrape down the sides and bottom of the bowl. On low speed, beat in the egg, vanilla, and almond extract until well incorporated, about 1 minute.

Add the flour mixture and mix until a little over half of it is incorporated. Stop the mixer and, using a sturdy silicone spatula or wooden spoon, mix in the milk chocolate, white chocolate, nuts, and coconut all at once. Mix just until no flour is visible and the chocolates, nuts, and coconut have been incorporated throughout the dough.

Roll heaping 1-Tbsp portions of dough and put them 3 in/7.5 cm apart on the prepared baking sheets.

Bake for 14 to 18 minutes, rotating the baking sheets halfway through, until the edges are lightly golden brown. Allow the cookies to sit on the baking sheets for 3 minutes, then transfer them to wire racks to cool completely before eating. The cookies will keep in an airtight container at room temperature for up to 3 days.

### note

I like to use sweetened (desiccated) coconut, but unsweetened works in a pinch.

### variation

Replace the milk chocolate chips with milk chocolate chunks, semisweet chocolate chips or chunks, or chopped dark chocolate (I find those with between 54 and 70 percent cacao to be best).

# CURIOUSLY CHEWY OATMEAL-RAISIN COOKIES

**MAKES ABOUT 48 COOKIES**

**Ah, if only I could have these cookies with me whenever I need some serious snackage! Just as their name says, they are curiously, wonderfully chewy. The batter is packed with raisins and makes enough cookies to last a family of serious snackers up to a week. The moment the cookies come out of the oven, you sprinkle them with cinnamon-sugar, bringing your chewy oatmeal-raisin cookie–eating experience to even greater heights.**

- **2 Tbsp granulated sugar, plus ½ cup/100 g**
- **2¾ tsp ground cinnamon**
- **1½ cups/180 g whole-wheat pastry flour or all-purpose flour**
- **¾ tsp baking soda**
- **½ tsp fine-grain sea salt**
- **1 cup/225 g unsalted butter, at room temperature**
- **1 cup/200 g packed light brown sugar**
- **2 large eggs, at room temperature**
- **1 tsp pure vanilla extract**
- **3 cups/300 g rolled oats (not quick-cooking)**
- **1¼ cups/210 g raisins**

Line two baking sheets with parchment paper.

In a small bowl, mix together the 2 Tbsp granulated sugar and 2 tsp of the cinnamon. Set this aside—it is for topping the cookies once they're out of the oven.

In a medium bowl, whisk together the flour, remaining ¾ tsp cinnamon, the baking soda, and salt. Set this aside.

In a large bowl with a handheld mixer or in the bowl of a stand mixer fitted with the paddle attachment, beat together the butter, brown sugar, and remaining ½ cup/100 g granulated sugar on medium speed for 3 to 5 minutes, until pale and creamy. Turn off the mixer and scrape the sides and bottom of the bowl. On low speed, beat in the eggs and vanilla until well incorporated.

Add the flour mixture and mix until just combined. Still on low speed, mix in the oats and raisins just until combined.

Cover the bowl with plastic wrap and put it in the refrigerator for 1 hour, or until the dough is firm.

Position two racks in the upper third and center of the oven. Preheat the oven to 350°F/180°C. Drop rounded 1-Tbsp portions of dough onto the prepared baking sheets, spacing them 2 in/5 cm apart.

Bake for 10 to 13 minutes, rotating the baking sheets halfway through baking, until the edges are golden and the tops look slightly underdone. Lightly sprinkle each cookie with some cinnamon-sugar. Allow the cookies to sit on the baking sheets for about 2 minutes before transferring them to wire racks to cool completely. The cookies will keep in an airtight container at room temperature for up to 3 days.

## variations

The raisins can be substituted with dried cranberries. If you're all about having a bit of crunch in your oatmeal cookies, use a mixture of raisins/dried cranberries and lightly toasted walnuts (simply roughly chop them, and add about ⅓ cup/35 g or as much as you feel is appropriate).

Don't like raisins? Use chocolate. If you'd prefer oatmeal chocolate chip cookies, substitute the raisins with about 1 cup/170 g chocolate chips or chopped dark chocolate (between 54 and 70 percent cacao, I feel, is ideal).

# PEANUT BUTTER PINNACLE COOKIES

**MAKES ABOUT 24 COOKIES**

**Ah, yes—another simple one-bowl recipe! I don't apologize for it, as these cookies are truly delectable despite their simplicity. The secret to making them really peanut buttery lies in the pinch of nutmeg and the bit of salt called for in the recipe; they make all the difference in the world in these absolutely straightforward cookies. Use either smooth or crunchy peanut butter—whichever you have on hand.**

**1¼ cups/150 g all-purpose flour**

**⅓ cup/65 g granulated sugar**

**¼ tsp fine-grain sea salt**

**⅛ tsp (a pinch, really) grated nutmeg**

**½ cup/115 g unsalted butter, at room temperature**

**⅓ cup/90 g smooth or crunchy peanut butter**

**2 egg yolks, at room temperature**

**Confectioners' sugar for dusting**

Position a rack in the middle of the oven. Preheat the oven to 350°F/180°C. Line a rimmed baking sheet with parchment paper.

In a large bowl using a handheld mixer or in the bowl of a stand mixer fitted with the paddle attachment, mix together the flour, sugar, salt, and nutmeg for about 15 seconds, or until combined. Add the butter, peanut butter, and egg yolks and mix on low speed until a dough ball forms (feel free to do all this in a food processor, using the pulse function).

Drop rounded 1-Tbsp portions of dough onto the baking sheet, spacing them 2 in/5 cm apart. Using the tines of a fork dipped in a bit of flour, press the rounds down, making a crosshatch pattern while flattening them slightly.

Bake for 10 to 13 minutes, until the cookies have just turned golden brown. Let the cookies cool for 3 minutes on the baking sheet, then transfer them to a wire rack to cool for 10 minutes. Serve with a dusting of confectioners' sugar on top. The cookies will keep in an airtight container at room temperature for up to 1 week.

# SAMEE COOKIES

**MAKES ABOUT 36 COOKIES**

**I'm told the very first cookie I ate was a vanilla wafer and throughout my childhood, instead of calling them by their proper name, I called them "Samee Cookies"—after my Aunt Samee, who introduced me to them. These Samee Cookies are vanilla wafers in almost every form, only they have a beautiful crackly exterior. The dough is simple to put together and can go straight from the mixing bowl to the oven. The cookies are best enjoyed completely cooled with a large glass of cold milk.**

**¾ cup/90 g all-purpose flour**

**1½ tsp baking powder**

**¼ tsp fine-grain sea salt**

**¼ cup/55 g unsalted butter, at room temperature**

**½ cup/100 g granulated sugar**

**1 Tbsp pure vanilla extract or vanilla bean paste**

**1 egg yolk**

Position a rack in the center of the oven. Preheat the oven to 350°F/180°C. Line a rimmed baking sheet with parchment paper.

In a medium bowl, whisk together the flour, baking powder, and salt. Set this aside.

In a large bowl using a handheld mixer or in the bowl of a stand mixer fitted with the paddle attachment, beat the butter on medium speed for about 2 minutes, until fluffy. Shut off the mixer, add the sugar, and beat on medium speed until the mixture is pale and fluffy, about 1 minute more. Scrape the sides and bottom of the bowl. On low speed, beat in the vanilla and egg yolk until just combined.

Add the flour mixture and mix until just combined.

Drop 1-tsp portions of dough onto the prepared baking sheet about 1 in/2.5 cm apart.

Bake for 15 to 18 minutes, until the cookies are crackly and lightly golden brown. Allow the cookies to cool for 2 minutes on the baking sheet before transferring them to a wire rack to cool completely. The cookies will keep in an airtight container at room temperature for up to 5 days.

# MOLASSES SPICE COOKIES

**MAKES 36 SMALL OR 12 LARGE COOKIES**

**The first time I had a molasses spice cookie was a couple of summers ago at a Mennonite bakery in Pennsylvania. The cookies were crispy-edged and chewy-bellied, and they tasted like Christmas in July. This is my version of those cookies; they're mighty fine to eat year-round; however, they are exceptional around the holidays.**

**2 cups/240 g all-purpose flour**
**1¾ tsp baking soda**
**1 tsp ground cinnamon**
**¾ tsp ground ginger**
**½ tsp ground cloves**
**½ tsp fine-grain sea salt**
**¾ cup/170 g unsalted butter, softened**
**½ cup/100 g packed dark brown sugar**
**½ cup/100 g granulated sugar**
**1 large egg, at room temperature**
**⅓ cup/75 ml molasses (not blackstrap)**
**½ cup/105 g turbinado or Demerara sugar**

In a medium bowl, whisk together the flour, baking soda, cinnamon, ginger, cloves, and salt. Set this aside.

In a large bowl using a handheld mixer or in the bowl of a stand mixer fitted with the paddle attachment, beat together the butter, brown sugar, and granulated sugar on medium speed until fluffy, about 3 minutes. Turn off the mixer and scrape the sides and bottom of the bowl.

On medium speed, beat in the egg and molasses until combined. Turn the speed to low and gradually add the flour-spice mixture just until a dough forms. Cover the bowl with plastic wrap and put it in the refrigerator for 2 hours, or overnight.

Once the dough has chilled, arrange two racks in the upper third and center of the oven. Preheat the oven to 350°F/180°C. Line two baking sheets with parchment paper. Put the turbinado sugar in a shallow bowl.

Evenly scoop 3 Tbsp of dough and form it into a round. Roll it in the turbinado sugar and put it on the baking sheet. Continue the scooping and rolling process, being sure to arrange the dough rounds 3 in/7.5 cm apart, as they do spread out a bit.

Bake, rotating the baking sheets halfway through, for 13 to 17 minutes, until the cookies are fairly flat and their edges are just firm. Let them cool on the baking sheets for about 5 minutes, then transfer them to wire racks to cool completely. The cookies will keep in an airtight container at room temperature for up to 1 week.

## notes

Because I am lazy when it comes to certain things, I like to make the dough a day ahead (which I believe helps the flavors mature a bit). And because I don't like washing dishes, I like to wrap the dough in plastic wrap a few times and put it on a plate, as the dough is very soft at this point.

For smaller cookies: If you prefer smaller, crispier-edged cookies, scoop 1-Tbsp portions of dough instead of the directed 3 Tbsp; just bake them for 10 to 15 minutes.

# NUTELLA SHORTBREAD SANDWICH COOKIES

**MAKES ABOUT 36 COOKIES**

**During my first semester of college, I carried around a plastic bag of shortbread cookies and a jar of Nutella to snack on during long breaks between classes. These shortbreads are great plain, dipped in hot milky tea, or consumed with your morning mug of coffee. And you can eliminate the mess of smearing the chocolate-hazelnut paste on the cookies as you go; instead, it's sandwiched right into these buttery treats.**

- **2½ cups/300 g all-purpose flour**
- **¼ tsp fine-grain sea salt**
- **1 cup/225 g unsalted butter, at room temperature**
- **1 cup/100 g confectioners' sugar**
- **1 tsp pure vanilla extract**
- **1 Tbsp milk**
- **Turbinado sugar for sprinkling**
- **Nutella for sandwiching between the cookies**

In a large bowl, whisk together the flour and salt. Set this aside.

In a large bowl using a handheld mixer or in the bowl of a stand mixer fitted with the paddle attachment, beat the butter on medium speed for about 2 minutes, until fluffy. Shut off the mixer, add the confectioners' sugar, and beat on medium speed until the mixture is pale and fluffy, about 1 minute more. Turn off the mixer and scrape the sides and bottom of the bowl. On medium speed, mix in the vanilla until just combined. Briefly stir in the flour-salt mixture. Add the milk and mix briefly, just until the dough holds together.

Form the dough into a disk, wrap it in plastic wrap, and put it in the refrigerator for about 1 hour, or until it has firmed up.

Position a rack in the center of the oven. Preheat the oven to 350°F/180°C. Line two baking sheets with parchment paper.

Roll out the dough on a lightly floured surface or between two pieces of parchment paper to ¼ in/6 mm thick. Cut it into rectangles, squares, rounds, or any other shape that you prefer.

Place the cookies on the prepared baking sheets, about 1 in/2.5 cm apart, and set them in the freezer for 15 minutes, or until the cookies have firmed up. The colder the dough, the better they'll keep their shape in the oven.

Sprinkle the dough with turbinado sugar and bake for about 10 minutes, or until the cookies have lightly browned. Let the cookies cool for 5 minutes on the baking sheets before transferring them to a wire rack. After the cookies have cooled, spread Nutella on half of the cookies and sandwich the plain cookies atop them. The cookies will keep in an airtight container at room temperature for up to 1 week.

# JAMMY LINZER COOKIES

**MAKES ABOUT 18 COOKIES**

**These cookies remind me of a fresh snowfall on Valentine's Day: They have heart-shaped centers and their tops are covered in a dusting of confectioners' sugar. But they're fit for any occasion—Christmas, Valentine's Day, or Mondays (Remember: Mondays always call for cookies). The ground hazelnuts in the cookies pair beautifully with the Back of a Napkin Strawberry Jam and are also great with lingonberry jam or black currant jam. Use a good jam that you'll enjoy eating, as it's the star of this lovely cookie.**

**2½ cups/185 g ground hazelnuts (see Note)**

**2½ cups/300 g all-purpose flour**

**½ tsp ground cinnamon**

**¼ tsp fine-grain sea salt**

**1 cup/225 g unsalted butter, at room temperature**

**1 cup/100 g confectioners' sugar, plus more for dusting**

**2 Tbsp cold milk, plus ½ Tbsp if needed**

**1 tsp pure vanilla extract**

**Back of a Napkin Strawberry or Raspberry Jam (page 107) or another jam of your choice**

In a medium bowl, whisk together the ground hazelnuts, flour, cinnamon, and salt. Set this aside.

In a large bowl using a handheld mixer or in the bowl of a stand mixer fitted with the paddle attachment, beat the butter on medium speed for about 2 minutes, until fluffy. Turn off the mixer, scrape down the sides of the bowl, and add the confectioners' sugar on medium speed until the mixture is pale and fluffy, about 1 minute. Turn off the mixture and scrape down the sides and bottom of the bowl. On medium speed, mix in the milk and vanilla until just combined.

Briefly stir in the ground nut–flour mixture until a ball forms. If the dough is dry, add the ½ Tbsp milk and mix briefly, just until the dough holds together.

Form the dough into two disks, wrap them in plastic wrap, and put them in the refrigerator for about 30 minutes, or until firm.

Arrange two racks in the upper third and center of the oven. Preheat the oven to 350°F/180°C. Line two baking sheets with parchment paper.

Roll one disk of dough on a lightly floured surface or between two sheets of parchment paper (lightly dust the parchment and the top of the dough with flour) to ¼ in/6 mm thick. Dip a 2-in/5-cm round (or fluted or plain—it's up to you) cookie cutter in flour and cut out rounds of dough, keeping the pieces as close to one another as possible. Transfer the cut dough to one of the prepared baking sheets, arranging the rounds about 1 in/2.5 cm apart. Using a smaller cookie cutter of your choice, cut out a small center from half of the cookie rounds.

Put the baking sheet in the freezer for 10 to 15 minutes, or until the cookies firm up. The colder the cookie dough, the better they'll keep their shape in the oven.

*continued*

While the dough chills, roll and cut out the rest of the dough as before. Put the chilled cookies in the oven and put this baking sheet in the freezer to allow the cookies to firm up as well.

Bake for 10 to 13 minutes, until the cookies are lightly browned around the edges. Let the cookies cool for 5 minutes on the baking sheet before transferring them to a wire rack to cool completely. Bake the next sheet of cookies.

After the cookies have cooled, dust the ones with the cut-out centers with confectioners' sugar and spread the other cookies with jam. Sandwich together. The cookies will keep in an airtight container at room temperature for up to 4 days.

## notes

To grind your own hazelnuts, simply put some hazelnuts into a food processor and pulse until they are mealy and fine; don't run the food processor for too long because you'll soon end up with hazelnut butter.

If the dough becomes very soft when you're rolling it, wrap it back in plastic wrap and refrigerate until it's manageable.

Keep in mind that once you've spread the jam on the crisp cookies, they begin to soften a bit.

## variation

Substitute other ground nuts for the hazelnuts (or use a combination); ground almonds and ground pecans work well.

# BACK OF A NAPKIN STRAWBERRY JAM

**MAKES ABOUT 1 CUP/325 G**

**The ingredients for this jam are simple enough to write on the back of a napkin.**

**1 lb/455 g fresh strawberries**
**1 cup/200 g granulated sugar**
**1 Tbsp cold salted or unsalted butter, cut into small cubes**

Put a couple of small plates in the freezer. Wash and hull the strawberries and halve them.

In a medium saucepan over medium heat, stir together the strawberries and sugar for 20 to 25 minutes, until thickened. To check if the jam is set, remove one chilled plate from the freezer and spoon a small dab of the mixture onto it. Give the jam about 30 seconds, and push it with your finger. If it wrinkles, it's set and done; if it moves about on the plate, it needs to be boiled a bit more before you test it on the other plate. You'll also know the jam is done when it reaches 210°F/100°C on a candy thermometer.

When the jam is set and done, remove it from the heat and stir in the butter. Skim off any foam from the surface with a metal spoon, then pour the jam into clean, heat-safe containers or jars. The jam will keep in the refrigerator for up to 2 weeks.

### variation

Add the juice of one medium lemon or the juice of half an orange to the strawberry mixture before cooking the jam to add a nice citrusy flavor and brighten the flavors of the berries.

# BACK OF A NAPKIN RASPBERRY JAM

**MAKES ABOUT 1 CUP/325 G**

**This is another easy-to-remember jam recipe: Just cook it for about 20 minutes and add the butter.**

**2 cups/250 g fresh raspberries**
**1 cup/200 g granulated sugar**
**1 Tbsp strained fresh orange juice**
**1 Tbsp finely grated orange zest**
**1 Tbsp cold salted or unsalted butter, cut into small cubes**

Put a couple of small plates in the freezer.

In a medium saucepan over medium heat, stir together the raspberries, sugar, orange juice, and orange zest for 20 to 25 minutes, until thickened and beautifully ruby red. To check if the jam is set, remove one chilled plate from the freezer and spoon a small dab of the mixture onto it. Give the jam about 30 seconds, and push it with your finger. If it wrinkles, it's set and done; if it moves about on the plate, it needs to be boiled a bit more before you test it on the other plate. You'll also know the jam is done when it reaches 210°F/100°C on a candy thermometer.

When the jam is set and done, remove it from the heat and stir in the butter. Skim off any foam from the surface with a metal spoon, then pour the jam into clean, heat-safe containers or jars. The jam will keep in the refrigerator for up to 2 weeks.

### variation

For blackberry jam, substitute blackberries for the raspberries and increase the amount of sugar to 1½ cups/300 g.

# GINGERBREAD PEOPLE

**MAKES 24 TO 48 SMALLISH GINGERBREAD PEOPLE**

**Growing up, I was never a fan of gingerbread; although I decorated my fair share of houses and cookies, eating the finished confection was never my thing. I always found it far too spicy. My tastes have matured, and I've grown to like gingerbread cookies—and these aren't too heavily spiced. These make beautifully delicious holiday decorations (feel free to use other shaped cutters besides the traditional kind for ornaments). If you plan to hang the decorated cookies on your tree or around the house, use a bamboo skewer to poke a hole in the top of the cookies as soon as they come out of the oven. After the cookies have cooled and you've decorated them, all you have to do is push string, ribbon, or metal ornament hangers through the holes.**

## COOKIES

**2 cups/240 g all-purpose flour**

**1 tsp ground ginger**

**½ tsp ground cinnamon**

**½ tsp grated nutmeg**

**¼ tsp baking soda**

**¼ tsp fine-grain sea salt**

**½ cup/115 g unsalted butter, at room temperature**

**⅓ cup/65 g packed dark brown sugar**

**1 large egg, at room temperature**

**¼ cup/85 g honey**

## ROYAL ICING

**1½ cups/150 g confectioners' sugar**

**1 egg white**

**1 tsp freshly squeezed strained lemon juice**

**5 Tbsp/75 ml boiling water**

**TO MAKE THE COOKIES:** In a medium bowl, whisk together the flour, ginger, cinnamon, nutmeg, baking soda, and salt. Set this aside.

In a large bowl using a handheld mixer or in the bowl of a stand mixer fitted with the paddle attachment, beat together the butter and sugar on medium speed for about 3 minutes, until light and fluffy. Turn off the mixer, scrape down the sides of the bowl, and add the egg on low speed until well incorporated, about 1 minute. Turn off the mixer and scrape down the sides and bottom of the bowl. On low speed, mix in the honey until combined.

With the mixer still running, pour in the flour-spice mixture and mix until everything comes together into a dough ball.

Form the dough into two disks, wrap them in plastic wrap, and put them in the refrigerator for at least 30 minutes, or until firm.

Meanwhile, position two racks in the upper third and center of the oven. Preheat the oven to 350°F/180°C. Line two rimmed baking sheets with parchment paper.

Roll one disk of dough between two sheets of parchment paper (lightly dust the parchment and the top of the dough with flour) to about ⅛ in/4 mm thick. Dip your cutter of choice in flour and cut out the gingerbread people. Transfer the cut dough to the prepared baking sheets. Repeat with the other disk of dough. Gather any dough scraps, chill them, and reroll as necessary.

*continued*

Bake for 10 to 13 minutes, rotating the baking sheets halfway through baking, until the cookies are a slightly darker shade than when they went into the oven and are ever-so-slightly puffed. Allow the cookies to cool completely on the baking sheets.

**TO MAKE THE ROYAL ICING:** In a medium bowl using a handheld mixer or in the bowl of a stand mixer fitted with the whisk attachment, beat the confectioners' sugar, egg white, and lemon juice until combined.

With the mixer still running, slowly stream in the boiling water and vigorously beat until the icing is well mixed and, when the beater is lifted, ribbons of icing fall back into the bowl.

Spoon the icing into a piping bag fitted with a fine tip, or put it in a large resealable plastic bag and cut off a tiny bit from one corner. Pipe desired designs onto the cooled gingerbread cookies. Allow the icing to harden before consuming. The decorated gingerbread people can be stored in an airtight container at room temperature for up to 2 weeks.

## notes

If the icing is too thick, loosen it with a bit more water; if it's runny, beat a little more and add a little more confectioners' sugar.

Once the icing is ready, you can stir in 1 tsp of a flavoring, leave it as it is, or divide the icing between bowls and stir in food colorings.

# ANIMAL CRACKERS

**MAKES ABOUT 3 CUPS/500 G OF COOKIES**

**My elementary school lunches were always interesting. The very second our hour-long break began, my friends and I would claim the long white table nearest the back of the cafeteria, empty our lunch boxes, and gather the undesirable bits of our meals to begin a businesslike exchange of food. First and foremost, vegetables were always tossed (no surprise there). Then we'd auction off and exchange the rest our food: cookies for small packets of Swiss rolls and chocolate milk for strawberry milk. We made a huge commotion, drawing kids from other tables to join in. The only thing that was nearly impossible to pry out of any kid's hand was a red rectangular box of animal crackers—back then, it was cool for seven-year-olds to walk around with animal-cracker boxes, even if they were empty. Over a decade later, my love for animal crackers is still strong. Good luck trying to pry a box of these babies out of my hands!**

**2 cups/240 g all-purpose flour**

**½ cup/70 g finely milled cornmeal**

**¾ tsp baking powder**

**¼ tsp ground allspice, or a pinch of mace and a pinch of nutmeg**

**¼ tsp salt**

**11 Tbsp/155 g unsalted butter, at room temperature**

**⅔ cup/130 g granulated sugar**

**1 large egg**

**½ tsp pure vanilla extract**

In a medium bowl, whisk together the flour, cornmeal, baking powder, allspice, and salt. Set this aside.

In a large bowl using a handheld mixer or in the bowl of a stand mixer fitted with the paddle attachment, beat together the butter and sugar on medium speed for about 3 minutes, until light and fluffy. Turn off the mixer and scrape down the sides of the bowl. On low speed, beat in the egg and vanilla until well incorporated, about 1 minute. Turn off the mixer and scrape down the sides and bottom of the bowl. Add the flour mixture and mix until a rough ball forms.

Form the dough into two disks, wrap them in plastic wrap, and put them in the refrigerator for about 1 hour, or until firm.

Position a rack in the center of the oven. Preheat the oven to 350°F/180°C. Line two rimmed baking sheets with parchment paper.

Roll one disk of dough between two sheets of parchment paper (lightly dust the parchment and the top of the dough with flour) to ⅛ in/4 mm thick. If the dough cracks while you're rolling it, allow it to sit at room temperature for about 5 minutes until it's a little easier to handle. Dip small, animal-shaped cookie cutters in flour and stamp them into the rolled-out dough, cutting the pieces as close to one another as possible. Transfer the dough to one of the prepared baking sheets, arranging the shapes about 1 in/2.5 cm apart. Put the baking sheet in the freezer for 15 minutes. Gather up any dough scraps, wrap in plastic wrap, and refrigerate.

Bake the chilled baking sheet for 13 to 16 minutes, until the cookies are a very light golden brown. Transfer the cookies immediately to a wire rack to cool completely. Roll, cut, and bake the remaining dough. The cookies will keep in a loosely covered container at room temperature for up to 1 week.

# GRAHAM CRACKERS

**MAKES 30 GRAHAM CRACKERS**

**Here's a recipe that might make you think I've gone mad: "First he wants me to make my own puff pastry, and now this?!" Of course! If you're nowhere near graham cracker land (formally known as North America), you probably have very limited access to these treats. And even if you live in North America, these crackers are definitely better than the store-bought variety. This recipe—no matter where you live—also lets you make both a great New York cheesecake (see page 174) and the perfect s'more. They're almost too good to make into a crust, and possibly too good to share, but for everyone's sake, I encourage you to do both!**

- **1 cup/140 g graham flour (see Note)**
- **1 cup/120 g all-purpose flour**
- **¾ cup/150 g packed dark brown sugar**
- **½ tsp fine-grain sea salt**
- **¼ tsp baking powder**
- **¼ tsp baking soda**
- **5 Tbsp/70 g cold unsalted butter, cut into ½-in/12-mm cubes**
- **¼ cup/85 g honey**
- **3 Tbsp cold milk**
- **4 tsp pure vanilla extract**

In a large bowl (or in the bowl of a food processor or stand mixer), mix together the graham flour, all-purpose flour, brown sugar, salt, baking powder, and baking soda until combined. With your fingertips, work the butter into the flours until the mixture resembles coarse crumbs. (If you're using a food processor, use the pulse function; if you're using a stand mixer, run it on medium-low speed.) Add the honey, milk, and vanilla and mix until a dough comes together. (If you're using a food processor or stand mixer, the dough will come together in a ball.)

Form the dough into two round disks, wrap them in plastic wrap, and put them in the refrigerator for 20 to 30 minutes, or until firm.

Roll one of the dough disks between two sheets of parchment paper (lightly dust the parchment and the top of the dough with flour) into an 11-by-9½-in/28-by-24-cm rectangle (it should be about 2 mm thick). While rolling the dough, lift the sheets of parchment every so often to prevent sticking and to smooth out any wrinkles in the dough.

Remove the top sheet of parchment paper and set it aside. Trim the edges of the dough to form an even rectangle.

Make three vertical cuts and five horizontal cuts in the dough (to make roughly 2-by-3-in/5-by-7.5-cm pieces); a ruler and a pizza cutter are helpful for this, but I often just eyeball it, using a sharp knife or fluted pastry wheel and the edge of a ruler as a straightedge rather than as a measuring implement.

To make your crackers look store-bought, use a sharp knife to cut each of the rectangles (lengthwise) in half, and neatly poke each half with a bamboo skewer or fork.

Transfer the dough, on its parchment, onto a rimmed baking sheet and chill it in the freezer for about 15 minutes.

Meanwhile, position a rack in the center of the oven. Preheat the oven to 350°F/180°C.

Bake for 11 to 15 minutes, until the edges of the graham crackers are golden brown. Using a knife (or a fluted pastry wheel), carefully cut through the large graham cracker rectangle to divide it into the smaller graham crackers.

Allow the crackers to cool on the baking sheet for 5 to 10 minutes, just until the baking sheet is cool to the touch. Transfer the crackers to a wire rack to cool completely before eating them (as they cool, the crackers will become crisp—as a graham cracker should be).

Repeat the process with the other half of the dough (use the reserved parchment and another sheet of parchment paper). The graham crackers will keep in an airtight container at room temperature for up to 10 days.

## notes

An alternative to the graham flour is 1 cup/125 g whole-wheat flour plus 1/4 cup/30 g wheat bran. It'll help you achieve a similar texture and flavor to graham flour.

If you're making graham crackers for the New York Cheesecake crust, there's no need for neatness—just roll out the dough to a thickness of 2 mm and haphazardly cut and poke it with a fork before baking.

# CRANBERRY AND ALMOND COCONUT MACAROONS

**MAKES 18 LARGE OR 36 SMALL MACAROONS**

**The inspiration for these coconut macaroons came during a two-hour wait at New York's Pennsylvania Station. I was walking in and out of stores, hoping to pass time. Then, as I walked through the doorway of a French bakery chain, I caught a glimpse of chocolate-covered macaroons. I immediately purchased one. It was crisp on the outside and soft in the center, and strewn throughout the mounded coconut cookie were chunks of ruby-red cranberries and bits of sliced almonds and chocolate—the most delicious way to kill time.**

**3 cups/360 g lightly packed shredded coconut (sweetened or unsweetened)**

**¾ cup/150 g granulated sugar**

**¾ cup/180 ml cold egg whites (from about 6 large eggs)**

**⅓ cup/55 g sweetened dried cranberries, roughly chopped, plus more for decorating**

**¼ cup/25 g sliced almonds, plus more for decorating**

**⅛ tsp fine-grain sea salt**

**⅛ tsp pure vanilla extract**

**⅛ tsp pure almond extract**

**2 oz/55 g chopped dark chocolate (optional)**

In a heavy 2- or 3-qt/2- or 2.8-L saucepan, combine the coconut, sugar, egg whites, cranberries, and almonds and stir well. Cook them over medium-low heat, stirring frequently, for 10 to 15 minutes. The mixture will look creamy as it heats and then it will slowly dry a bit, with individual flakes of coconut becoming discernible.

Stop cooking when it no longer looks creamy but is still quite sticky and moist. Remove the pan from the heat and stir in the salt, vanilla, and almond extract. Scrape the mixture into a small baking dish, spread it out, and allow it to cool at room temperature (or put in the refrigerator for about 30 minutes).

Position a rack in the center of the oven. Preheat the oven to 300°F/150°C. Line a rimmed baking sheet with parchment paper.

Using your hands, scoop and firmly pack the coconut mixture into small domes, about 2 Tbsp each. A medium bowl of warm water for swishing your hands is helpful to have around. Space each dome evenly on the prepared baking sheet 1 in/2.5 cm or so apart.

Bake until the macaroons are a nice light golden, 27 to 33 minutes.

Put the baking sheet on a wire rack until it is completely cool. Remove the macaroons from the baking sheet and set them on the rack. Put the rack over the baking sheet.

Melt the chocolate (if using) in a heatproof bowl over a pan of gently simmering water. (Or, melt it in the microwave for about 1 minute, stirring every 10 seconds until the chocolate is completely melted.)

Drizzle the melted chocolate over the macaroons. Sprinkle on some sliced almonds and/or cranberries if you want, and that's all she wrote. The macaroons, before drizzling with chocolate, will keep in an airtight container in the refrigerator for up to 5 days, and for 1 to 2 months in the freezer; just drizzle on the melted chocolate before serving.

# PISTACHIO POLVORÓNES

**MAKES ABOUT 36 COOKIES, AFTER YOU'VE EATEN A BIT OF THE COOKIE DOUGH**

**After the chocolate chip cookie, polvorónes might be my second favorite type of cookie. They're a crumbly Spanish shortbread most popularly known as Mexican wedding cookies or Russian tea cakes. There are many variations, but ideally a polvorón is crumbly, not cloyingly sweet, and always mixed with some type of nut, traditionally pecans or walnuts. The cookie also needs a good balance of texture and flavor. Most important, it should crumble when you bite into it—this is one of the major signs that you've made a good polvorón.**

- **1 cup/120 g all-purpose flour**
- **1 cup/120 g whole-wheat pastry flour (see Note)**
- **¼ tsp ground cinnamon**
- **¼ tsp fine-grain sea salt**
- **1 cup/225 g unsalted butter, at room temperature**
- **2¼ cups/225 g confectioners' sugar**
- **1½ tsp pure vanilla extract**
- **½ tsp pure almond extract**
- **¾ cup/95 g shelled unsalted dry-roasted pistachios (see Note), half roughly chopped and half coarsely ground**
- **¼ cup/20 g almond meal**

In a large bowl, whisk together the all-purpose flour, pastry flour, cinnamon, and salt.

In a large bowl using a handheld mixer or in the bowl of a stand mixer fitted with the paddle attachment, beat the butter on medium speed for about 2 minutes, until fluffy. Turn off the mixer, add ¾ cup/75 g of the confectioners' sugar, and beat on medium-low speed, until the mixture is pale and fluffy, about 1 minute more. Turn off the mixer and scrape the sides and bottom of the bowl. On medium speed, mix in the vanilla and almond extract until just combined.

On low speed (or using a sturdy wooden spoon or silicone spatula), slowly add the flour mixture until just combined. All at once, briefly mix in the pistachios and almond meal. Cover the bowl with plastic wrap. Put the dough in the refrigerator for at least 30 minutes, or until it is firm.

Position a rack in the upper third of the oven. Preheat the oven to 350°F/180°C. Line a baking sheet with parchment paper.

Roll the dough into 1-Tbsp rounds and coat each round well with some of the remaining 1½ cups/150 g confectioners' sugar (you definitely will not use all of it in this step, but you will need the remainder later, so don't throw it away). Put each round on the prepared baking sheet 1 in/2.5 cm apart and put it in the freezer for about 15 minutes, until the dough rounds are firm.

Bake, rotating the baking sheet halfway through, until the cookies are cracked and lightly blushed with gold all around the edges, 18 to 22 minutes.

Allow the cookies to sit on the baking sheet for 10 minutes, then carefully transfer them to a wire rack to cool completely. Once thoroughly cooled, roll each cookie in the remaining confectioners' sugar, being sure to shake off any excess. The cookies will keep in an airtight container in a cool place for up to 5 days.

*continued*

## notes

No whole-wheat pastry flour? You can easily substitute it with an equal amount of all-purpose flour. I simply like to use a combination of all-purpose flour and whole-wheat pastry flour because the latter enhances the nuttiness of the cookies.

If you can't find *unsalted* dry-roasted pistachios (unshelled, of course), I wouldn't worry; simply reduce the amount of salt to ⅛ tsp, and all should be well!

## variation

I take some liberties with the concept of these polvorónes, nodding to the suspected Levantine origins of these Latin cookies by using a mixture of pistachio nuts and almond meal instead of the traditional pecans or walnuts. An equal amount of lightly toasted pecans or walnuts or, if you prefer, more almond meal, should work well in place of the pistachios.

# EVERYDAY BROWNIES

**MAKES 9 TO 16 BROWNIES**

**These brownies are insanely chocolatey and somewhat fudgy, but hold their shape like a proper brownie should, and the chocolate flavor is intensified and sharpened by help of the brown sugar and salt in the recipe (brownie purists, trust me on this—you won't regret it). These come together in scarcely more time than a brownie mix, which makes them perfect to make on any day, especially if you have a busy schedule or a last-minute gathering to attend. They store beautifully in the freezer for snacking on a whim, and they're also great to have in a lunch box. A large glass of cold milk is obligatory no matter which way you have them.**

- 1 cup/225 g unsalted butter
- 1½ cups/300 g natural cane sugar or granulated sugar
- ⅓ cup/65 g packed dark brown sugar
- 1⅓ cups/130 g unsweetened cocoa powder (natural or Dutch-processed)
- ½ tsp fine-grain sea salt
- 2 tsp pure vanilla extract
- 3 large eggs, cold (see Note)
- ¾ cup/90 g whole-wheat pastry flour or all-purpose flour
- 5 oz/150 g roughly chopped dark chocolate (54 to 70 percent cacao; optional but recommended)
- 1 cup/115 g toasted walnut or pecan pieces (optional), roughly chopped

Position a rack in the upper third of the oven. Preheat the oven to 325°F/165°C. Line an 8-in/20-cm square baking pan with parchment paper or aluminum foil, leaving an overhang around each side.

In a medium saucepan, melt the butter over low heat. With a wooden spoon or sturdy silicone spatula, mix in the cane sugar, brown sugar, cocoa powder, and salt. At this point, the mixture should be lukewarm. If it's not, set it aside for 5 minutes or so until a clean finger can comfortably stay in the mixture without getting burned. (Everything will be gritty at this point; worry not!)

Vigorously stir in the vanilla and eggs. Once the batter appears shiny and the eggs are blended in well, add the flour all at once, mixing only until the flour has disappeared. If you're adding in the chocolate and nuts, briskly stir them into the batter. Spread the batter evenly into the prepared pan.

Bake for 38 to 43 minutes, until a toothpick plunged into the center emerges slightly moist with batter.

Allow the brownie to cool slightly in the pan, then transfer the pan to a wire rack to cool completely. Lift the ends of the parchment liner and transfer the brownie block to a cutting board. Cut it into 16 squares (or into 9 squares if you want bigger brownies). The brownies will keep in an airtight container at room temperature for up to 1 week, or for 6 months in the freezer (they're always finished long before then in my house).

continued

## note

The secret to the moistness of these brownies is the cold eggs; if you prefer a brownie that's a little less moist and a little more cakey, use room-temperature eggs and briefly beat them with a whisk before adding them to the batter. Once the batter is ready to be baked, tag on a couple more minutes of baking time.

If you freeze the brownies with any chocolate or nut mix-ins, let them thaw for 5 minutes or so before snacking right out of the freezer, as the shards of frozen chocolate and nuts can be quite difficult to bite into.

## variation

I highly recommend mixing the optional dark chocolate into the batter for this recipe; if you're not big on dark chocolate, use a milk chocolate instead, or a less-intense dark chocolate such as one with about 54 percent cacao.

# FUDGY FLOURLESS CHOCOLATE BROWNIES

**MAKES 16 TO 25 BROWNIES**

**Brownie purists might shoot me down in flames after reading that I use brown sugar in my brownies. So be it! With this luscious batter, there simply must be a generous amount of rich, dark muscovado sugar. These brownies bake into fudge-bellied morsels that are rich and satisfying. I tested and shared these with many friends, and everyone agreed that I should tell you to cleave to the recipe as much as possible because it is lovely.**

- **1 cup/225 g cold unsalted butter, cubed**
- **8 oz/225 g good-quality dark chocolate (62 to 72 percent cacao; see Note), roughly chopped**
- **¾ cup/150 g natural cane sugar or granulated sugar**
- **¼ cup/50 g packed dark muscovado sugar or brown sugar (see Note)**
- **1 Tbsp pure vanilla extract**
- **¼ tsp fine-grain sea salt**
- **3 large eggs, cold (see Note, page 125)**
- **1¾ cups/140 g almond meal, passed through a sieve (see Note)**
- **½ cup/70 g dry roasted unsalted macadamia nuts (see Note), chopped**
- **½ cup/65 g dry roasted shelled unsalted pistachio nuts (see Note), chopped, plus 1 Tbsp chopped dry roasted pistachio nuts (optional) for sprinkling**

Position a rack in the upper third of the oven. Preheat the oven to 350°F/180°C. Line an 8-in/20-cm square baking pan with parchment paper or aluminum foil, leaving an overhang around each side.

In a medium saucepan, melt the butter and chocolate together over low heat into a smoothly amalgamated mixture. Remove the pan from the heat and, with a wooden spoon or sturdy silicone spatula, mix in the cane sugar, muscovado sugar, vanilla, and salt.

Allow the mixture to cool for 5 to 10 minutes, just until a clean finger can comfortably stay in the mixture without getting burned. (Everything will be gritty at this point; worry not!) Vigorously stir in the eggs, one at a time, along with the almond meal, macadamias, and pistachios. Spread the batter evenly into the prepared pan. Bake for 25 to 30 minutes, until the mixture is set and isn't wobbly. The top will be light in color and soft to the touch. Because these are quite fudge-bellied, a cake tester is of no use, as the brownies come out wet, even when they are done.

Allow the brownie to cool completely in the pan on a wire rack, cover with foil, then put the pan in the freezer for 20 minutes. This will allow for easy, clean cutting. Lift the ends of the parchment liner and transfer the brownie block to a cutting board. Sprinkle with the 1 Tbsp chopped pistachios for added texture. Cut it into 16 to 25 squares. The brownies will keep in an airtight container at room temperature for up to 1 week.

continued

## notes

Good-quality chocolate makes all the difference in the taste of these brownies, so use an excellent brand such as Valrhona, Callebaut, El Rey, Sharffen Berger, Green & Black's, Lindt, Endangered Species Chocolate, or Nói Síríus.

The recipe calls for melting the butter and chocolate together; doing so will prevent the chocolate from burning. However, if you are still wary of burning the chocolate, go ahead and melt both ingredients together in a large heatproof bowl over a saucepan of simmering water.

If you're a brownie purist or would rather not include the dark muscovado or brown sugar, increase the amount of natural cane sugar or granulated sugar to 1 cup/200 g, and leave the brown sugar out.

Go ahead and use another kind of ground nut in place of the almond meal: walnut meal, hazelnut meal, or pecan meal all work well.

I adore the combination of macadamia nuts and pistachio nuts in these brownies. They're both rather pricey, which makes these brownies appropriate for special occasions, but you can definitely use 1 cup/115 g of any of your favorite chopped nut or a combination. Do note that if all you can find are salted nuts, completely leave out the salt called for in the recipe; if all you can find is salted pistachio nuts in their shells, simply reduce the salt to ⅛ tsp.

# NANCY DREW BLONDIES

**MAKES 16 TO 36 BLONDIES, DEPENDING ON HOW GREEDY YOU FEEL**

**These blondies are named after the teenage detective in the series of mystery novels that my mother read as a child. In the movie starring Emma Roberts, Nancy Drew used these treats as a tool of bribery; though they make great bribes, these are just as perfect for sharing. The original Nancy Drew blondies, as I've found out, are only walnut-flecked. Surely you can go that route with these blondies; however, I also like to stir milk chocolate chips and white chocolate chips into the batter, which make for irresistible blondies worthy of sharing and even for bribing.**

- **6 Tbsp/85 g cold unsalted butter**
- **1 cup/200 g packed light brown sugar or muscovado sugar**
- **1½ tsp pure vanilla extract**
- **¼ tsp salt**
- **1 large egg, cold (see Note, page 125)**
- **1 cup/120 g whole-wheat pastry flour or all-purpose flour**
- **½ cup/85 g white chocolate chips**
- **½ cup/85 g milk chocolate chips**
- **⅓ cup/35 g walnuts, lightly toasted and roughly chopped (optional)**

Position a rack in the upper third of the oven. Preheat the oven to 350°F/180°C. Line an 8-in/20-cm square baking pan with parchment paper or aluminum foil, leaving an overhang around each side.

In a medium saucepan, melt the butter over low heat. Remove the pan from the heat and with a wooden spoon or sturdy silicone spatula, mix in the brown sugar, vanilla, and salt until smooth and lump free. Quickly stir in the egg until well incorporated. Add the flour, white chocolate chips, milk chocolate chips, and walnuts (if using) all at once. Stir the mixture until just incorporated. Spread the batter evenly into the prepared pan.

Bake for 25 to 30 minutes, until the mixture is golden, set in the middle, and a toothpick or cake tester plunged into the center comes out clean or with a few stray crumbs attached.

Allow the blondie to cool completely in the pan. Lift the ends of the parchment liner and transfer the blondie block to a cutting board. Cut it into 16, 25, or 36 squares. I prefer to err on the side of 36, as these are quite rich, and they're good for snacks at that size. The blondies will keep in an airtight container at room temperature for up to 5 days.

## variations

Instead of using chips, chop up chunks of white chocolate and milk chocolate from bars. If you're not into either white or milk chocolate, you can leave them out and increase the amount of toasted walnuts to 1 cup/115 g. If you're not into walnuts, use pecans or any kind of nut you feel to be appropriate.

zero
lb/kg
OXO

# piece of cake

signed my receipt and slid it across the counter. Sarah, my best friend, stood next to me, laughing. "You still sign your name the same way you did in middle school!" I asked, "I do?" She smiled. "Yep. It's still the same." That's Sarah for you—she remembers the smallest details of our lives nearly a decade ago.

"Oh, do you remember that essay we wrote for Mr. Feldman's class?" she asked. I took a moment to flip through my old memories. "Barely, I think."

"Well, you wrote about food. So typical of you!" It really is.

Mr. Feldman was our seventh-grade English teacher (and in the eighth grade, our history teacher). We read a lot and had real-life, mature conversations in his classes. He was the kind of teacher everyone wants to have: He hated tests and quizzes and found them unnecessary, but he did believe in projects and writing. One day, he told my class to write an essay about ourselves; I don't specifically remember what the essay called for, but I do remember the topic offered us a lot of wiggle room—making it more difficult than easy, as we first thought. I spent days gathering my thoughts on paper—splicing together important pieces of who I was in just a few paragraphs. Eventually every idea on the page was tossed aside, and I decided to write about food—in particular, cake.

Cake baking, to me, is an art form. And many other people believe it to be that, too. If my seventh-grade self—a child lacking in dexterity and height—could make cakes, I think you'll be fine. Don't let the fear of a botched cake from the past scare you now. Cake baking, simply, is just this: Mix some simple ingredients together, pour it into a lined pan, and put it in the oven.

I'm not going to go all "This is easy! You can't screw it up!" on you, because there's always room for mess-ups, and even the most experienced bakers ruin their cakes sometimes. Such is life, and if your cake falls you can always make a trifle out of it.

As I mentioned at the beginning of the book (see page 17), check your ingredients for freshness, especially your leavening agents—eggs, baking soda, and baking powder. A tip on testing eggs: If you place them in a bowl of water, and one bobs up and down or feels half empty in the shell, toss it—it's a bad egg. All the recipes in this section require large eggs at room temperature; it's essential in cake baking to allow everything to mix together properly and to allow for proper rising of the cakes.

Even I often forget to take the eggs out to sit at room temperature, so to avoid waiting insane amounts of time, I sit them in a bowl of very warm tap water. Other times, I'll just let warm tap water run over the eggs for a couple of minutes. But the prior method is best, especially if boiling-hot water comes out of your faucets. It's instant or near-instant gratification.

"Room-temperature" butter is not ice-cold, but should yield when you press on it with a finger; it shouldn't be mushy like creamy mashed potatoes.

The cakes that follow use various mixing techniques—some are one-bowl recipes, some utilize a method made popular by the queen of baking science, Rose Levy Beranbaum, and others are classic mixing methods.

# INSANELY MOIST CHOCOLATE CUPCAKES

**MAKES 16 CUPCAKES**

**I find nearly every excuse possible not to dirty another bowl or spoon while baking, so I'm happy to say that this recipe doesn't require much cookware. It's a batter that can be made with one bowl and a silicone spatula. It can also be made using a stand mixer (which I find to be a bit more work) or a food processor. Although they are effortless to put together, these cupcakes are of the finest breed—they are incredibly moist and flavorful, just as a chocolate cupcake should be.**

- **1 cup/200 g natural cane sugar or granulated sugar**
- **¾ cup plus 2 Tbsp/105 g all-purpose flour**
- **¼ cup plus 2 Tbsp/30 g unsweetened cocoa powder (natural or Dutch-processed)**
- **¾ tsp baking powder**
- **¾ tsp baking soda**
- **½ tsp fine-grain sea salt**
- **1 large egg, at room temperature**
- **½ cup/120 ml sour cream, at room temperature**
- **¼ cup/60 ml sunflower oil**
- **1 Tbsp pure vanilla extract**
- **½ cup/120 ml boiling water**
- **Easy Cocoa Frosting (page 136)**
- **Chocolate shavings and/or sprinkles, for decorating (optional)**

Position a rack in the upper third of the oven. Preheat the oven to 350°F/180°C. Line two standard muffin tins with 16 paper liners.

In a large heatproof mixing bowl, carefully whisk together the sugar, flour, cocoa powder, baking powder, baking soda, and salt until there aren't any visible lumps. Crack in the egg, spoon in the sour cream, and pour in the sunflower oil and vanilla. Briefly mix with a wooden spoon or silicone spatula (I prefer the latter) just until smooth and combined.

Pour in the boiling water and slowly mix, starting from the center and working your way outward (this trick makes it easy to mix without splattering batter everywhere). The batter will be quite liquid, but this is normal.

Divide the batter evenly among the lined cups, using the silicone spatula to assist with bowl scraping. Fill each lined cup about halfway with 3 Tbsp batter.

Bake for 15 to 19 minutes (being sure to carefully rotate the tins halfway through baking), until a cake tester or a wooden toothpick inserted into the center of a cupcake comes out clean.

Transfer the tins to wire racks for about 10 minutes, until the tins are cool to the touch. Remove the cupcakes and transfer them to the racks. Let the cupcakes cool completely before frosting them and decorating with chocolate shavings (if using). The cupcakes will keep in an airtight container at room temperature for up to 2 days.

### note

To frost the cupcakes, use a small offset spatula (or a butter knife without a serrated edge) at an angle to spread the frosting smoothly around the cake. To create the indent in the center like that in the photo, use a large cake spatula and turn 360 degrees one way, and then turn 180 degrees in the opposite direction; lift the spatula, and that's it!

# EASY COCOA FROSTING

**MAKES 2 CUPS/640 G; ENOUGH TO FROST 16 TO 24 CUPCAKES OR 1 CAKE LAYER**

**I've tried making this in the same saucepan in which the butter is melted, adding all the ingredients to the butter, but the heat of the pan is far too intense for the confectioners' sugar and other ingredients and makes the frosting split. You want the heat of the melted butter to dissolve the sugar, but you don't want to make everything a big mess. You could let both the pan and the butter cool, but then the butter won't be hot enough to properly dissolve the sugar. A room-temperature bowl and hot butter—it's the only way.**

- **9 Tbsp/130 g unsalted butter, melted**
- **¾ cup/75 g unsweetened cocoa powder (natural or Dutch-processed)**
- **6 Tbsp/90 ml whole milk, plus more as needed**
- **3⅓ cups/340 g confectioners' sugar, plus more as needed**
- **1½ tsp light corn syrup or golden syrup**
- **1¼ tsp pure vanilla extract**

In a large bowl using a handheld mixer or in the bowl of a stand mixer fitted with the paddle attachment, combine the butter and cocoa powder until smooth. Now, mix in the milk and confectioners' sugar to achieve a spreading consistency. Mix in the corn syrup and vanilla. Add another 1 Tbsp or so of milk or confectioners' sugar if necessary to adjust the consistency. Allow the frosting to sit for 10 minutes to thicken a bit, and use as needed.

# CHOCOLATE SWISS ROLL

**MAKES ONE 9-BY-5-IN/23-BY-12-CM ROLL**
**SERVES 4 TO 6**

There's a reason that Swiss rolls (also known as jelly rolls or Yule logs) are a classic. They're easy to make and are great for dinner parties or spur-of-the-moment cake hankerings. Be prepared to get a kitchen towel dirty; use a clean one that you don't mind staining with cocoa.

- ½ cup/60 g all-purpose flour
- ½ cup/50 g unsweetened cocoa powder (natural or Dutch-processed), sifted, plus more for dusting
- ¾ tsp baking powder
- 4 large eggs plus 1 egg yolk, at room temperature
- Pinch of fine-grain sea salt
- ½ cup plus 2 Tbsp/125 g granulated sugar
- ¼ cup/55 g unsalted butter, melted and slightly cooled
- ½ recipe Billowy Whipped Cream (page 65)
- Confectioners' sugar for dusting (optional)
- Berries of your choice for adorning the cake (optional)

Position a rack in the center of the oven. Preheat the oven to 450°F/230°C. Grease the bottom and sides of a 9-by-13-in/23-by-33-cm baking pan and line with parchment paper. Grease the top of the parchment and dust the pan with cocoa powder; tap out the excess.

In a medium bowl, whisk together the flour, cocoa powder, and baking powder. Set this aside.

In a large bowl using a handheld mixer or in the bowl of a stand mixer fitted with the whisk attachment, whisk together the eggs, egg yolk, and salt on high speed until thick and doubled in volume, about 3 minutes. With the mixer still on, steadily stream in all the granulated sugar; continue mixing on high speed for another 3 minutes, or until the mixture is light in color and thick in consistency, and leaves a trail when the whisk is lifted out. You shouldn't be able to feel granules of sugar when you press a dot of the mixture between your thumb and forefinger.

With a spatula, carefully sprinkle the flour-cocoa mixture on top of the egg mixture. Gently fold it in until just incorporated. Stream the butter down the side of the bowl, carefully stirring just to bring everything together.

Pour the mixture into the prepared pan and gradually tilt the pan back and forth so the mixture levels out and evenly spreads into the corners.

Bake for 7 to 10 minutes, or until the cake begins to pull away from the edges of the pan, the cake is springy to the touch, and a cake tester inserted into the center of the cake comes out clean or with a few crumbs attached.

While the cake bakes, evenly dust a clean tea towel or flour sack towel (it should be longer than the pan) with cocoa powder. Once the cake is baked, run a thin knife along the sides, then invert the cake onto the prepared towel. Carefully loosen and peel off the parchment from the bottom of the warm cake.

continued

Working quickly, trim the edges of the cake with a sharp knife just enough to square everything off, then make a score 1 in/2.5 cm from one of the shorter edges, being sure not to cut more than halfway through (this will help the cake to roll neatly). Lightly dust the top of the cake with more cocoa powder.

Put a clean piece of parchment or wax paper on the dusted cake (skip this if you like living on the edge, but I like to take proper precautions). Firmly roll up the warm cake from the cut end, including the tea towel, and leave the cake to cool completely; doing so will make the cake easier to fill later. Put the rolled package in a loaf pan to help it hold its shape, and set it in the refrigerator to cool for at least 2 hours.

Once the cake is cool, carefully unroll it. Remove the sheet of parchment and evenly spread the whipped cream onto the cake, leaving a ½-in/12-mm border all around. Re-roll the cake (without the tea towel inside the cake, of course), dust with more cocoa or some confectioners' sugar, top with a few blackberries or raspberries (if desired), and serve. This cake is best served the same day it's made.

### note

For the perfectionist in all of us: Instead of serving the filled cake right away, wrap the tea towel around the cake, and secure it with metal binder clips or clothespins to help maintain the shape of the filled roll. Transfer the wrapped roll to a baking sheet and allow it to rest in the refrigerator for up to 3 hours before serving.

# FLOURLESS CHOCOLATE CAKE

**MAKES ONE 9-IN/23-CM SINGLE-LAYER CAKE; SERVES 6 TO 8**

**If someone were to bake me a cake on my birthday, this would be the one I would want the most. It's dense, custard-like, and extraordinarily chocolaty. Once baked, the cake begins to crackle and fall in the center, which only adds to its gloriously winsome appearance. After a rest in the refrigerator, the cake is embellished with snow-white drapery and plump jewels—here, in the form of Billowy Whipped Cream and jet-black berries.**

- **6 large eggs**
- **1 cup/225 g cold unsalted butter, cut into cubes**
- **7 oz/200 g dark chocolate, roughly chopped**
- **1 cup/200 g granulated sugar**
- **1/3 cup/30 g unsweetened cocoa powder (natural or Dutch-processed), sifted**
- **1 Tbsp pure vanilla extract**
- **1/4 tsp fine-grain sea salt**
- **3/4 cup/180 ml boiling water**
- **1/2 recipe Billowy Whipped Cream (page 65)**
- **Berries of your choice and grated orange zest for adorning the cake (optional)**

Separate the eggs, placing the yolks in a small, clean bowl and the egg whites in a large, clean bowl. Set both bowls aside.

Position a rack in the center of the oven. Preheat the oven to 350°F/180°C. Grease the bottom of a 9-in/23-cm springform pan and line with parchment paper. Grease the parchment and dust the pan with cocoa powder; tap out the excess.

In a heavy-bottom medium saucepan over low heat, melt together the butter and chocolate. Remove the pan from the heat and, using a wooden spoon or sturdy silicone spatula, mix in the sugar, cocoa powder, vanilla, and salt; stir until the batter is smooth and free of any lumps. Mix in the egg yolks until well combined, and slowly stir in the boiling water.

With a whisk or a handheld mixer, vigorously beat the large bowl of egg whites until thick and billowy, like cappuccino foam (or, for those more technically inclined, until they form medium peaks).

Take about one-third of the foamy egg whites and vigorously beat them into the chocolate batter. With a spatula or large metal spoon, gently fold in the remaining egg whites until they are no longer visible in the batter. Immediately pour the batter into the prepared pan.

Bake for 43 to 47 minutes, until the cake is firm and crackly on top.

Allow the cake to cool in the pan on a wire rack for about 1 hour. Cover with a double layer of plastic wrap and transfer the pan to the refrigerator for 4 hours, or overnight.

Run a knife around the inside of the pan to help release the cake from the edges. Remove the cake from the pan and set on a serving plate. Drape the whipped cream over the top and decorate it with a handful of your favorite berries and a sprinkling of orange zest (if desired) before serving. The undecorated cake will keep in an airtight container in the refrigerator for up to 4 days.

### *variations*

If you prefer, use a combination of dark chocolate and milk chocolate.

Instead of whipped cream, top the cake with 1 recipe Classic Chocolate Ganache (page 148).

# EVERYDAY CHOCOLATE CAKE

**MAKES ONE 9-IN/23-CM SINGLE-LAYER CAKE; SERVES 4 TO 6**

**You needn't get out any spatulas to frost this cake—just scoop the frosting over the top of the cooled moist cake, casually spread it around with a butter knife, and slice into it.**

**1 cup/200 g natural cane sugar or granulated sugar**

**¾ cup plus 2 Tbsp/105 g all-purpose flour**

**¼ cup plus 2 Tbsp/30 g unsweetened cocoa powder (natural or Dutch-processed)**

**¾ tsp baking powder**

**¾ tsp baking soda**

**½ tsp fine-grain sea salt**

**½ cup/120 ml sour cream, at room temperature**

**¼ cup/60 ml sunflower oil**

**1 large egg, at room temperature**

**1 Tbsp pure vanilla extract**

**½ cup/120 ml boiling water or black coffee (if you have any left over from breakfast)**

**1 recipe Easy Cocoa Frosting (page 136)**

Position a rack in the center of the oven. Preheat the oven to 350°F/180°C. Butter a 9-in/23-cm round cake pan and line with parchment paper. Butter the parchment and dust the pan with flour or cocoa powder; tap out the excess.

In the bowl of a food processor, pulse together the sugar, flour, cocoa powder, baking powder, baking soda, and salt until combined.

Add the sour cream, sunflower oil, egg, and vanilla, then pour in the boiling water and pulse until everything is just combined. Pour the batter into the prepared pan.

Bake for 30 to 35 minutes, until the cake is springy and pulls away from the sides of the pan and a cake tester inserted into the center of the cake comes out clean or with a few stray crumbs attached.

Remove the cake from the oven and use a clean oven mitt (preferably a cloth one) to gently press down on the middle of the cake to make it level. Doing this allows you to skip the usual step of trimming the cake.

Transfer the pan to a wire rack to cool for 20 minutes. Invert the cake onto the rack and peel off the parchment. Re-invert the cake and let it cool completely.

Once the cake is completely cooled, transfer it to a cake plate, the bottom of a tart tin, or a large plate. Spread the frosting over the top of the cake and serve. The cake will keep, covered, at room temperature for up to 3 days.

*continued*

### note

This is practically the same recipe as the Insanely Moist Chocolate Cupcakes (page 134), so if you don't have a food processor, you can mix by hand or in a stand mixer. The results are just as great!

### variations

Some like them tall: If you'd like a layer cake, double the recipes for both the cake and the frosting, then fill the center with Back of a Napkin strawberry or raspberry jam (see page 107) or your favorite prepared jam.

Add some pizzazz: Another great version of this cake would be one made with the zest of half an orange (1 tsp or thereabouts; 2 tsp zest if doubling the recipe) added to the batter, then adorned with chocolate frosting and candied orange peel.

Another option: For a one-layer peanut butter and chocolate cake, frost the cake with Peanutty Peanut Butter Frosting (at right) and pour on a Classic Chocolate Ganache (page 148).

# PEANUTTY PEANUT BUTTER FROSTING

**MAKES A LITTLE OVER 1 CUP/250 G; ENOUGH TO FROST A 9-IN/23-CM SINGLE-LAYER CAKE**

**The ultimate secret to making things particularly peanut buttery is the addition of nutmeg and salt. Though the amounts called for are quite small, they enhance the peanut flavors admirably. This frosting is heavenly sandwiched between shortbread cookies (see page 102) or Peanut Butter Pinnacle Cookies (page 96) and is great for topping cakes and smearing onto brownies.**

- **1 cup/270 g smooth peanut butter**
- **¼ cup/55 g unsalted butter, at room temperature**
- **1 cup/100 g confectioners' sugar**
- **¼ tsp fine-grain sea salt**
- **¼ tsp grated nutmeg**
- **1 Tbsp whole milk or heavy (whipping) cream**
- **1 tsp pure vanilla extract**

In a large bowl using a handheld mixer or in the bowl of a stand mixer fitted with the paddle attachment, beat together the peanut butter and butter on low speed until well mixed.

Turn off the mixer, scrape down the sides of the bowl, and add the confectioners' sugar, salt, and nutmeg. Turn the mixer to low speed and mix until everything is well incorporated. With the mixer still running, beat in the milk and vanilla until combined throughout. Use immediately, as needed.

### note

For added texture in the frosting, use crunchy peanut butter or stir ⅓ cup/45 g honey-roasted unsalted peanuts.

# YELLOW BIRTHDAY CAKE

**MAKES ONE 8-IN/20-CM DOUBLE-LAYER CAKE; SERVES 10 TO 12**

**Yes, this is a yellow cake prettified with Easter-yellow frosting and sprinkles, but with a secret layer of chocolate ganache in the middle. It is the kind of cake you make for someone who likes chocolate but isn't keen on chocolate cake. The mixing technique is a little unusual for this cake; it was created by Rose Levy Beranbaum (I must give credit where credit is due), and I find it creates a cake with a rich, moist, close crumb, which allows for thinnish slices to be doled out without feeling cheap.**

**1½ cups/180 g all-purpose flour**

**1½ cups/185 g cake flour**

**1¾ cups/350 g granulated sugar**

**1 Tbsp baking powder**

**½ tsp fine-grain sea salt**

**1 cup/225 g unsalted butter, at room temperature, cut into 1-in/2.5-cm cubes**

**1¼ cups/300 ml whole milk, at room temperature**

**4 large eggs, at room temperature**

**1 Tbsp pure vanilla extract**

**Water Ganache (recipe follows) or Classic Chocolate Ganache (page 148)**

**Easy Vanilla Buttercream (page 148)**

**Fresh edible organic flowers, (see Note, page 151), candies, or sprinkles for decoration**

Position a rack in the upper third of the oven. Preheat the oven to 350°F/180°C. Butter two 8-in/20-cm or 9-in/23-cm round cake pans and line with parchment paper. Butter the parchment and dust the pans with flour; tap out the excess.

In the bowl of a stand mixer fitted with the paddle attachment, combine the all-purpose flour, cake flour, sugar, baking powder, and salt and mix on low speed for about 15 seconds, until combined. Add the butter pieces, mixing until they are just coated with flour; the mixture will be pebbly.

In a large bowl or measuring cup, whisk together the milk, eggs, and vanilla. With the mixer on medium speed, add the wet ingredients in three parts, scraping down the sides of the bowl before each addition. Beat the mixture until the ingredients are incorporated, but be sure not to overbeat. Evenly divide the batter between the prepared cake pans and smooth out.

Bake for 25 to 35 minutes, rotating the pans halfway through, until the cakes are golden brown, pull away from the sides, and a cake tester inserted into the center of each cake comes out clean or with a few stray crumbs attached.

Remove the cakes from the oven and use a clean oven mitt (preferably a cloth one) to gently press down on the middle of the cakes to make them level. Doing this allows you to skip the usual step of trimming the cakes.

Transfer the pans to wire racks to cool for 20 minutes. Invert the cakes onto the racks and peel off the parchment. Re-invert the cakes and let them cool completely.

Put one cake layer on a cake board or stand (bottom-side up) and spread on the ganache, being sure not to spread it all the way to the edges. Leave at least a ½-in/12-mm border at the edge. Place the second cake on top of the first (bottom-side up).

*continued*

At this point, put the cake layers in the refrigerator for 20 minutes or the freezer for 10 minutes, which will make frosting the cake much easier and will prevent the cake from buckling as you work with it.

Using an offset spatula, spread a thin layer of buttercream over the top and sides of the cake. Let it set in the refrigerator for 20 to 30 minutes. Remove the cake and spread a thick coat of the remaining frosting over the base coat. Decorate as desired and serve. The cake will keep, covered, at room temperature for up to 3 days.

### note

A couple of ideas: The cake is beautiful when it's adorned with edible flowers or sprinkles or simply decorated with the frosting. Of course, you don't have to use a vanilla frosting; you could choose to fill and decorate the cake with Easy Cocoa Frosting (page 136; double the recipe) or Classic Chocolate Ganache (page 148; double this as well).

## WATER GANACHE

**MAKES 1 CUP/125 G; ENOUGH TO FROST A SINGLE-LAYER CAKE; DOUBLE THE RECIPE FOR CUPCAKES OR A DOUBLE-LAYER CAKE**

**Because this recipe uses no cream or milk that could take away from the flavors of the chocolate, be sure to use a good chocolate (the best you can afford). If you like, use piping-hot tea instead of boiling water.**

**½ cup/120 ml boiling water**

**5 oz/140 g good-quality dark chocolate (62 to 70 percent cacao), finely chopped**

In a heatproof bowl, pour the boiling water over the chocolate. Swirl the bowl so that all the water heats and melts all the chocolate. Allow it to stand for a minute once all the chocolate has melted. Whisk the mixture until it is smooth and glossy (the chocolate might seize up or get hard and separate, but this is normal—just keep whisking until it's smooth).

The mixture will be runny. Set it aside and whisk it every now and again until it cools, after which the mixture will thicken significantly. Use immediately, as needed.

# CLASSIC CHOCOLATE GANACHE

**MAKES 1 CUP/240 ML; ENOUGH TO FROST ONE SINGLE-LAYER CAKE**

**Ganache is a standard French chocolate spread for cake and other desserts. This recipe is simple and always works. You may use 1 cup/170 g of semisweet chocolate chips instead of bar chocolate, but keep in mind that the quality of the chocolate you use will make a difference in the taste of the final product.**

**8 oz/225 g chopped dark chocolate (54 to 70 percent cacao)**

**1 cup/240 ml heavy (whipping) cream**

**½ tsp light corn syrup or golden syrup**

Put the chocolate in a medium heatproof bowl. In a small saucepan over medium heat, bring the heavy cream to a simmer. Remove the pan from the heat and pour the cream over the chocolate. Let the mixture sit for a minute, then stir it until it's smooth.

Allow it to sit at room temperature until it is thick. Stir in the corn syrup, and use the ganache as needed. This can be made 1 day ahead and stored in the refrigerator covered with plastic wrap. Bring to room temperature before using.

# EASY VANILLA BUTTERCREAM

**MAKES 2 CUPS/650 G; ENOUGH TO FROST ONE DOUBLE-LAYER CAKE**

**A simple buttercream, this comes together in a snap.**

**4 cups/400 g confectioners' sugar**

**10 Tbsp/140 g unsalted butter, at room temperature**

**¼ cup/60 ml whole milk**

**1 Tbsp pure vanilla extract**

**Food coloring of your choice (optional)**

In the bowl of a stand mixer fitted with the paddle attachment, beat all the ingredients together on low speed until well combined. Set this aside until you're ready to decorate the cake.

# CARIBBEAN PRINCESS CAKE

**MAKES ONE 6-IN/15-CM DOUBLE-LAYER CAKE; SERVES 8**

I'm not into breathtakingly precious-looking cakes covered in fondant or elaborately piped frosting. I prefer a good handmade cake that is simply decorated and utterly flavorful. However, this cake is one fit for the princess in your life—Caribbean or not.

The cake gets its "Caribbean" tag from the fact that it's simply a classic Dominican cake (made a little simpler, I might add). Dominican cakes are by far some of the most exquisite that anyone can partake in—they're moist, tender-crumbed, and sandwiched with guava, pineapple, or dulce de leche. Recipes for such well-crafted cakes are safeguarded by many Dominican bakers. The cakes are often sold by the pound; this makes a ½-lb/225-g cake.

## CAKE

**2⅔ cups/320 g all-purpose flour**

**1 Tbsp baking powder**

**1 tsp fine-grain sea salt**

**1 cup/225 g unsalted butter, at room temperature**

**1 cup/200 g granulated sugar**

**4 large eggs plus 2 egg yolks, at room temperature**

**½ cup/120 ml whole milk**

**2 tsp pure vanilla extract (use Dominican if you can find it)**

## GUAVA FILLING

**¼ cup/60 g guava paste**

**1 Tbsp granulated sugar**

**White Meringue Frosting (page 152)**

**Fresh edible organic flowers (see Note), candlies, or sprinkles for decorating**

**TO MAKE THE CAKE:** Position a rack in the upper third of the oven. Preheat the oven to 350°F/180°C. Butter two 6-by-2-in/15-by-5-cm round cake pans and line with parchment paper. Butter the parchment and dust the pans with flour; tap out the excess.

In a medium bowl, whisk together the flour, baking powder, and salt. Set aside.

In a large bowl using a handheld mixer or in the bowl of a stand mixer fitted with the paddle attachment, beat together the butter and sugar on medium speed for about 6 minutes, until light and fluffy, scraping down the sides of the bowl as needed.

Turn the mixer speed to low and add the eggs and egg yolks, one at a time. Add the milk and vanilla and beat until incorporated. With the mixer still running, add the flour mixture and mix just until the flour is no longer visible. Evenly divide the batter between the prepared cake pans and smooth it out.

Bake for 44 to 48 minutes, rotating the pans halfway through baking, until the cakes are golden brown, pull away from the sides, and a cake tester inserted into the center of each cake comes out clean or with a few stray crumbs attached.

Remove the cakes from the oven, and use a clean oven mitt (preferably a cloth one) to gently press down on the middle of the cakes to make them level. Doing this allows you to skip the usual step of trimming the cakes.

*continued*

Transfer the pans to wire racks to cool for 20 minutes. Invert the cakes onto the racks and peel off the parchment. Re-invert the cakes and let them cool completely.

**TO MAKE THE FILLING:** In a small saucepan over medium heat, combine the guava paste, ¼ cup/60 ml water, and the sugar and stir the mixture continuously until it reaches spreading consistency, about 4 minutes. Set the saucepan aside.

Put one cake layer on a cake board or stand (bottom-side up) and spread on the guava filling, being sure not to spread it all the way to the edges. Leave at least a ½-in/12-mm border at the edge. Place the second cake on top of the first (bottom-side up).

At this point, put the cake layers in the refrigerator for 20 minutes or the freezer for 10 minutes, which will make frosting the cake much easier and will prevent the cake from buckling as you work with it.

Using an offset spatula, spread a thin layer of the meringue over the top and sides of the cake. Let it set in the freezer for 20 to 30 minutes. Remove the cake and spread a thick coat of the remaining frosting over the base coat. Decorate it with fresh edible flowers and serve. The cake will keep, sliced and separated with baking parchment, in an airtight container in the refrigerator for up to 3 days.

## notes

You can use 9-by-2-in/23-by-5-cm round cake pans; be sure to check cakes 10 minutes earlier for doneness.

Be sure to buy fresh, edible, organic flowers to decorate the cake. Flowers that aren't organic might harbor harmful pesticides that could make you sick.

## variations

Don't like guava? Instead of using the guava filling, fill the cake with about ¼ cup/60 ml of Dulce de Leche (page 152).

If you prefer a pineapple filling: In a medium saucepan over medium heat, combine ¼ cup/60 g crushed canned pineapple, 2 Tbsp juice from the canned pineapple, ¼ cup/50 g granulated sugar, and a pinch of fine-grain sea salt. Cook until the mixture is the consistency of thick maple syrup. Let it cool completely before using.

# WHITE MERINGUE FROSTING

**MAKES ABOUT 4 CUPS/400 G; ENOUGH TO FROST ONE DOUBLE-LAYER CAKE OR 24 CUPCAKES**

This meringue frosting is great for cupcakes or on a layer cake. Go ahead and flavor it with extracts other than vanilla and add vibrancy to it with food coloring.

- ½ cup/120 ml egg whites (from about 4 large eggs)
- 1 cup/200 g granulated sugar
- 1½ tsp fresh lemon or lime juice
- 2 tsp pure vanilla extract
- ¼ tsp fine-grain sea salt
- Food coloring (optional)

Fit a large heatproof bowl over a saucepan of gently simmering water (the water should not touch the bowl). Put all the ingredients in the bowl along with 3 Tbsp water and continuously whisk the mixture (either by hand or with a handheld mixer) until it feels hot to the touch and is no longer gritty. The sugar should be completely dissolved and everything should look satiny, which will take about 3 to 4 minutes.

Remove the bowl from the simmering water and, using either a handheld mixer or a stand mixer fitted with the whisk attachment, beat the mixture on high speed until it is cool to the touch and stiff and glossy, 6 to 8 minutes. Stir in a drop or two of your favorite food coloring, or leave as-is and use as needed. Best if used right away.

# DULCE DE LECHE

**MAKES 1¼ CUPS/300 ML; ENOUGH TO FILL ONE DOUBLE-LAYER CAKE AND HAVE PLENTY LEFT OVER FOR ICE CREAM**

Dulce de leche is a rich, sweet, caramel-like sauce that can be used for all things sweet. It's ideal sandwiched between cake layers such as in the Caribbean Princess Cake (page 149) and is heavenly on top of ice cream. This method is very simple: Boil a can (or a few, if you want more) of sweetened condensed milk submerged in water for two hours, after which you let the can cool completely before opening. It doesn't require very much effort to make.

- One 14-oz/400-g can sweetened condensed milk

Put the can of condensed milk in a heavy-bottom medium saucepan. Submerge the can completely in water and bring the water to a boil over high heat; decrease the heat to medium-high and leave the water on a constant light boil, topping off the pan with water as needed, for 2 hours. Be sure not to let the water completely evaporate as this might cause a huge mess in your kitchen. After 2 hours of boiling, allow the can to cool completely before opening and using.

### note

If you'll feel more at ease, use a large pot of water to submerge the can (or multiple cans if you want to have more dulce de leche on hand). The cooking time will be the same; just remember to top the pot off with water every now and again.

# TRES LECHES (THREE MILKS) CAKE

**MAKES ONE 9-IN/23-CM SINGLE-LAYER CAKE; SERVES 6 TO 8**

This is as moist and irresistible as a simple cake can get. It might sound strange to cover a cake in three types of milk—over 1 qt/960 ml total—but it does this cake good. You might think that after absorbing so much liquid, the cake would collapse and fall into pieces; instead, it retains the milks, making it moist and delicious. All it needs is a languorous draping of Billowy Whipped Cream, but go ahead and festoon the top with a couple large handfuls of your favorite fruit as well.

The charm of this cake not only lies in its moistness but in the fact that it's meant to be served straight out of the pan. I like to use parchment to line the bottom of the pan—though it gets soggy, of course, it helps to prevent any unwanted scratching of the pan that might occur through cutting and serving the cake, which is important.

## CAKE

1 cup/120 g all-purpose flour

3/4 cup/100 g cake flour

2 tsp baking powder

1/2 tsp fine-grain sea salt

3/4 cup/170 g unsalted butter, at room temperature

1 cup/200 g granulated sugar

3 large eggs plus 2 egg yolks, at room temperature

4 tsp pure vanilla extract

## GLAZE

2 1/4 cups/540 ml whole milk

One 14-oz/400-g can sweetened condensed milk

3/4 cup/180 ml buttermilk

1/2 recipe Billowy Whipped Cream (page 65)

Fresh fruit and/or edible flowers (see Note, page 151; optional)

**TO MAKE THE CAKE:** Position a rack in the center of the oven. Preheat the oven to 350°F/180°C. Grease a 9-in/23-cm square baking pan and line with parchment paper.

In a medium bowl, whisk together the all-purpose flour, cake flour, baking powder, and salt; set aside.

In a large bowl using a handheld mixer or in the bowl of a stand mixer fitted with the paddle attachment, beat together the butter and sugar on medium speed for about 6 minutes, until light and fluffy. Turn off the machine and scrape down the sides of the bowl with a silicone spatula.

Turn the mixer speed to low and add the eggs and egg yolks, one at a time. Beat in the vanilla. With the mixer still running, add the flour mixture and mix just until the flour is no longer visible. Turn off the mixer and scrape down the sides of the bowl, making sure no flour has settled to the sides and bottom. If it has, simply stir it in until it disappears into the batter. Pour the batter into the prepared cake pan and smooth it out, being sure to get the batter into the corners.

*continued*

Bake for 25 to 30 minutes (rotating the pan halfway through baking), until the cake is golden brown, pulls away from the sides, and a cake tester inserted into the center of the cake comes out clean or with a few stray crumbs attached.

**TO MAKE THE GLAZE:** Whisk together the whole milk, condensed milk, and buttermilk in a large measuring cup or medium bowl. Put the bowl, covered, in the refrigerator until the cake is out of the oven.

Remove the cake from the oven and use a strand of dry spaghetti or a bamboo skewer to poke all over the cake (being sure to pierce it to the bottom). Allow the cake to cool completely in the pan on a wire rack (or in the refrigerator if you prefer).

Once the cake is cooled, give the milk mixture a quick whisk and evenly pour all of it on the cooled cake. Cover the pan with plastic wrap, put it in the refrigerator, and allow it to sit for a couple of hours, until the entire mixture has been absorbed by the spongy cake.

Spread the whipped cream atop the cake and garnish with your favorite fruits, if desired, before serving. The cake will keep, covered with plastic wrap, in the refrigerator for up to 4 days.

# LEMON–POPPY SEED DRIZZLE CAKE

**MAKES ONE 9-IN/23-CM BUNDT CAKE; SERVES 6 TO 8**

**Four words: lemony lip-puckering goodness. This cake is for every card-toting lemon lover out there. It's very bold and doesn't skimp a bit on the citrus flavor. I make it for my sister, Sabrina, a picky eater and a disliker of chocolate in almost every form, but a true lover of lemons.**

## CAKE

**1½ cups/180 g all-purpose flour**

**1 cup/200 g granulated sugar**

**3 Tbsp poppy seeds**

**2 tsp baking powder**

**¾ tsp fine-grain sea salt**

**10 Tbsp/150 g unsalted butter, at room temperature, cut into ½-in/12-mm cubes**

**½ cup/120 ml whole milk, at room temperature**

**3 large eggs, at room temperature**

**4½ tsp finely grated lemon zest (from 3 large unwaxed lemons)**

## SYRUP

**1½ cups/150 g confectioners' sugar**

**⅓ cup/75 ml strained fresh lemon juice (from the 3 zested lemons)**

**TO MAKE THE CAKE:** Position a rack in the upper third of the oven. Preheat the oven to 350°F/180°C. Butter and flour the entire inside of a 9-in/23-cm Bundt or tube pan; tap out the excess flour.

In a large bowl using a handheld mixer or in the bowl of a stand mixer fitted with the paddle attachment, combine the flour, granulated sugar, poppy seeds, baking powder, and salt. Mix on low speed until combined, about 15 seconds. Add the butter, mixing until the pieces are just coated with flour. The mixture will be pebbly.

In a large bowl or measuring cup, whisk together the milk, eggs, and zest. With the mixer speed on medium, add the liquid to the flour in three parts, being sure to scrape down the sides of the bowl after each addition. Beat the mixture until the ingredients are incorporated, about 1 minute; be careful not to overbeat. Pour the batter into the prepared pan.

Bake for 30 to 35 minutes, until the cake is golden brown on top, pulls away from the sides, and a cake tester inserted into the center of the cake comes out clean or with a few stray crumbs attached.

Let the cake cool in the pan for 15 minutes on a wire rack.

**TO MAKE THE SYRUP:** In a small saucepan over medium-low heat, whisk together the confectioners' sugar, lemon juice, and ⅓ cup/75 ml water until the sugar has dissolved and the entire mixture is liquid. Be careful that the mixture doesn't come to a boil. Remove from the heat immediately.

After the cake has cooled in its pan, run a small spatula or butter knife around the inside of the cake and around the middle tube, and invert the cake onto a cake plate with a raised edge or small metal pizza pan. It should still be a bit warm.

Use a strand of dry spaghetti or a bamboo skewer to prick the entire top of the cake, then dribble the lemon syrup evenly over the cake.

Let the cake cool completely before serving. The cake will keep, covered, in the refrigerator, for up to 3 days.

# CARROT CAKE

**MAKES TWO 8-BY-4-IN/20-BY-10-CM LOAF CAKES OR ONE 6-IN/15-CM DOUBLE-LAYER CAKE; SERVES 8 TO 10**

**This is the only carrot cake recipe you'll need. Like the Apple Harvest Loaf Cake (page 164), this cake benefits from being wrapped as it cools overnight, which allows the flavors of the cake to come out. Feel free to halve the recipe to make a one-layer cake or one loaf cake.**

**1 cup/120 g whole-wheat pastry flour or all-purpose flour**

**1 tsp baking powder**

**1 tsp baking soda**

**Heaping 1 tsp ground cinnamon**

**Scant ½ tsp fine-grain sea salt**

**1½ cups/165 g coarsely grated carrots, at room temperature**

**1½ tsp finely grated orange zest**

**¼ cup/60 ml sunflower oil (or any neutral-tasting oil like vegetable or canola)**

**1 cup/200 g natural cane sugar or granulated sugar**

**¼ cup/60 ml organic full-fat plain yogurt, at room temperature**

**2 large eggs, at room temperature**

**3 recipes Tangy Cream Cheese Frosting (page 28)**

Position a rack in the center of the oven. Preheat the oven to 350°F/180°C. Butter and flour (or line with parchment) two 8-by-4-in/20-by-10-cm loaf pans or two 6-in/15-cm round cake pans.

In a medium bowl, whisk together the flour, baking powder, baking soda, cinnamon, and salt.

In another bowl, mix together the carrots and orange zest.

In a large bowl, using a spatula or whisk, combine the sunflower oil and sugar until all the sugar is coated with oil. Whisk in the yogurt until the mixture is smooth. Add the eggs, one at a time, beating until the batter is smooth. Add the flour mixture to the egg mixture and stir evenly. Gently stir in the carrot mixture. Evenly divide the batter between the prepared pans.

Bake for 30 to 45 minutes (err closer to 45 minutes if you're baking 6-in/15-cm layer cakes; aim for 30 to 35 minutes for loaf cakes), rotating the pans halfway through baking, until the cakes are well risen and firm to the touch and a cake tester inserted into the center comes out clean or with a few stray crumbs attached.

Cool the cakes in their pans on wire racks.

Frost the cakes, cover with plastic wrap, and put them in the refrigerator for 24 hours before serving.

### notes

No trimming required: If making a layer cake, once the cakes are out of the oven, use a clean oven mitt or kitchen towel to firmly press on the tops of the cakes to flatten out the domes, then allow them to cool. To make a cake as pictured on page 163, after frosting it, gently press handfuls of shredded coconut (sweetened or unsweetened) onto the sides of the cake.

Pan options: Instead of using 6-in/15-cm round cake pans as I did, you can use two 8-in/20-cm round cake pans (you can get away with 9-in/23-cm round cake pans, too, if that's all you have). Just be sure to check the cakes around 30 minutes.

Try mixing in ½ cup/60 g shredded coconut (sweetened or unsweetened), ¼ cup/25 g coarsely chopped pecans, ¼ cup/25 g coarsely chopped walnuts, or 2 Tbsp finely chopped dried sweetened cranberries with the carrots and orange zest for additional flavor and texture.

# APPLE HARVEST LOAF CAKE

**MAKES ONE 9-BY-5-IN/23-BY-12-CM LOAF CAKE; SERVES 4 TO 6**

This cake is meant to be made during the middle of autumn, at the peak of apple season. It is warm and moist and tastes like autumn sunrises, fallen leaves, and cool breezes. The ingredient list is quite lengthy, but the beauty of this loaf cake is that everything comes together in a large mixing bowl and there's no need to peel the apples—just chop them small and mix everything together with a spoon. Serve with salted butter or honeyed almond butter, a few thin apple slices, and a cup of warm cider, tea, or coffee.

## TOPPING

**2 Tbsp rolled oats (not quick-cooking)**

**1 Tbsp packed light muscovado sugar or dark brown sugar**

**Heaping ¼ tsp ground cinnamon**

**Pinch of grated nutmeg**

**Pinch of fine-grain sea salt**

## CAKE

**1 cup/120 g all-purpose flour**

**1 cup/80 g almond meal**

**½ cup/100 g natural cane sugar or granulated sugar**

**⅓ cup/65 g packed light muscovado sugar**

**⅓ cup/30 g rolled oats (not quick-cooking)**

**1 Tbsp ground cinnamon**

**2½ tsp baking powder**

**1¼ tsp fine-grain sea salt**

**¾ tsp ground ginger**

**½ tsp grated nutmeg**

**⅓ cup/75 ml thick plain yogurt (e.g., Greek yogurt; nonfat is okay), at room temperature**

**⅓ cup/75 ml milk, at room temperature**

**5 Tbsp/70 g unsalted butter, melted**

**1 large egg, at room temperature**

**2 cups/200 g cored chopped McIntosh apples (roughly ⅓-in/8-mm pieces)**

**½ cup/35 g walnut pieces, toasted and roughly chopped**

**¼ cup/40 g dried cranberries or golden raisins**

**TO MAKE THE TOPPING:** In a small bowl, mix together the oats, muscovado sugar, cinnamon, nutmeg, and salt. Set this aside.

**TO MAKE THE CAKE:** Position a rack in the center of the oven. Preheat the oven to 350°F/180°C. Line the bottom of a 9-by-5-in/23-by-12-cm loaf pan with parchment paper.

In a large bowl, mix together the flour, almond meal, cane sugar, muscovado sugar, oats, cinnamon, baking powder, salt, ginger, and nutmeg. Set this aside.

In a medium bowl, whisk together the yogurt, milk, butter, and egg. Mix the yogurt mixture into the flour mixture until just combined.

Briefly stir the apples, walnuts, and cranberries into the batter. Pour the batter into the prepared loaf pan and evenly sprinkle the reserved topping over the loaf.

Bake for 50 to 55 minutes, until the loaf is set on top, pulls away from the sides, and a cake tester inserted into the center of the loaf comes out clean.

Immediately cover the pan with aluminum foil, and let the cake rest at room temperature for 8 to 12 hours (see Note). The cake will keep, covered, at room temperature for up to 3 days.

## note

This loaf cake is not your usual kind. It's easy to put together, but it does require some time in the form of waiting. There's a bit of resting involved, which only betters the flavors of the cake. But even I don't follow my own directions sometimes, so if you lack the patience to let the cake rest (covered) overnight, or if you're short on time, let the cake cool in the pan for about 20 minutes or thereabouts, and then slice right in.

## variation

Make it special: This loaf cake tastes like apple pie and carrot cake met, fell in love, and made a baby. It's warm like spicy apple pie and almost carrot cake–like in moistness and crumb; instead of topping the cake with the smattering of oats and sugary spices, a nice smearing of Tangy Cream Cheese Frosting (page 28) would be fabulous.

# BANANA BREAD

**MAKES ONE 9-BY-5-IN/23-BY-12-CM LOAF CAKE; SERVES 4 TO 6**

**My very first memory of school was of warm banana bread, cold milk, and lots and lots of crying. I was four or five at the time, and couldn't part from my parents. Although all the other five-year-olds were pretty calm and collected, I grabbed on to my father's leg, teary-eyed. I was cajoled into entering the brick building and I was walked to a long white speckled table, where a container of milk and a warm slice of banana bread awaited me on a white Styrofoam tray. I liked school immediately.**

## CAKE

**2 cups/240 g all-purpose flour**

**1 cup/200 g granulated sugar**

**1½ tsp baking powder**

**1 tsp baking soda**

**1¼ tsp fine-grain sea salt**

**⅔ cup/165 ml full-fat plain yogurt, at room temperature**

**½ cup/115 g unsalted butter, melted**

**2 large eggs, at room temperature**

**1 Tbsp pure vanilla extract**

**3 large ripe bananas, peeled and mashed (see Note)**

## TOPPING

**⅓ cup/30 g rolled oats (not quick-cooking)**

**4 tsp dark brown sugar**

**Scant 1 tsp ground cinnamon**

**Pinch of fine-grain sea salt**

**1 ripe banana, peeled and cut in half lengthwise**

**TO MAKE THE CAKE:** Position a rack in the center of the oven. Preheat the oven to 300°F/150°C. Butter a 9-by-5-in/23-by-12-cm loaf pan, or line with parchment paper.

In a large bowl, whisk together the flour, granulated sugar, baking powder, baking soda, and salt. Using a wooden spoon or a sturdy silicone spatula, mix in the yogurt, butter, eggs, and vanilla until well incorporated, about 1 minute. Stir in the mashed bananas until well combined, about 30 seconds. Pour the mixture into the prepared pan and spread it evenly, making sure to get the batter into the sides of the pan.

**TO MAKE THE TOPPING:** Combine the oats, brown sugar, cinnamon, and salt in a small bowl. Evenly pour the mixture on top of the batter, then adorn the top with the sliced banana.

Bake for 60 to 65 minutes, until a cake tester inserted into the center of the loaf comes out clean or with a few stray crumbs attached.

Allow the loaf to cool in the pan on a wire rack for 10 to 15 minutes until the pan is cool enough to handle. Turn out the loaf and dole out warm slices. The loaf will keep, covered, at room temperature for up to 3 days.

## notes

To mash the bananas, put the peeled bananas on a large plate or cutting board and smash them one at a time with the tines of a fork, working your way from one end to the other. If you have a potato ricer, you can use that, too.

You might note that the banana bread sinks down—this is because of the halved banana placed on the top of the batter; you can skip the banana topping altogether and just top the cake with the handful of oats and cinnamon-sugar, or completely skip that, too.

# BROOKLYN CRUMB CAKE

**MAKES ONE 9-IN/23-CM CAKE; SERVES 6 TO 8**

**Brooklyn is known for its fantastic crumb cake. Call this what you may—crumb cake, coffee cake, crumb-coffee cake—it's a tender, moist sour cream–butter cake covered in an avalanche of flavorful, soft crumb topping. I don't skimp on the crumb topping here because it is, after all, a crumb cake.**

## TOPPING

**1½ cups/180 g all-purpose flour**

**½ cup/100 g packed dark brown sugar**

**⅓ cup/65 g packed light brown sugar**

**1 Tbsp ground cinnamon**

**¼ tsp fine-grain sea salt**

**½ cup/115 g unsalted butter, melted**

**1½ tsp pure vanilla extract**

## CAKE

**2 cups/240 g all-purpose flour**

**¾ cup/150 g granulated sugar**

**½ tsp fine-grain sea salt**

**½ tsp baking powder**

**¼ tsp baking soda**

**½ cup/115 g unsalted butter, at room temperature, cut into 16 slices**

**¾ cup/180 ml sour cream, at room temperature**

**1 large egg plus 1 egg yolk, at room temperature**

**1 tsp pure vanilla extract**

**Confectioners' sugar for sprinkling**

**TO MAKE THE TOPPING:** In a medium bowl, whisk together the flour, both brown sugars, the cinnamon, and salt. Stir the butter and vanilla into the flour mixture just until it becomes coarse and crumbly. Set this aside.

**TO MAKE THE CAKE:** Position a rack in the center of the oven. Preheat the oven to 325°F/165°C. Butter a 9-in/23-cm square baking pan and line the bottom and sides with parchment paper, leaving some overhang for easy transporting once baked.

In a large bowl using a handheld mixer or in the bowl of a stand mixer fitted with the paddle attachment, mix together the flour, granulated sugar, salt, baking powder, and baking soda on low speed for about 15 seconds. With the mixer still running, add the butter pieces, mixing until they're just coated with flour. The mixture will be pebbly.

With the mixer on medium speed, add the sour cream until it's just incorporated. Scrape the sides of the bowl with a silicone spatula; add the egg, egg yolk, and vanilla; and beat until everything is just incorporated.

Scrape the batter into the prepared baking pan and smooth it out, being sure to get it into the corners. Squeeze together handfuls of the topping mixture and scatter them across the batter, being sure to break large crumbs into smaller ones but making the crumbs of various sizes. Gently pat each handful into the batter.

Bake for 60 to 65 minutes, until the cake is golden brown, pulls away from the sides of the pan, and a cake tester inserted into the center of the cake comes out clean or with a few stray crumbs attached.

Allow the cake to cool completely in the pan on a wire rack. Cut it into squares and sprinkle the top with confectioners' sugar. The cake will keep in an airtight container at room temperature for up to 5 days.

# EVER-SO-CLASSY PAVLOVA

**MAKES ONE 8-IN/20-CM DESSERT; SERVES 4 TO 6, OR 3 ADDICTS**

**This pavlova is as classy as the ballerina for whom the dessert was named. The recipe is quite simple, but it is fit for any occasion because it is so beautiful. The outside of the pavlova meringue is slightly crisp, but its inside is soft, marshmallow-like, and as billowy as the whipped cream used to top the confection. Here I've covered the top in a duvet of Billowy Whipped Cream, several handfuls of halved strawberries, passion fruit, and a smattering of coarsely chopped pistachio nuts, but dress your pavlova to fit your tastes.**

- 5 egg whites, at room temperature
- 1¼ cups/250 g granulated sugar
- Pinch of fine-grain sea salt
- 1¼ tsp white vinegar
- 1 recipe Billowy Whipped Cream (page 65)
- Fruit of your choice (blackberries, raspberries, blueberries, passion fruit, strawberries, etc.), for garnish
- Chopped pistachio nuts or another nut of your choice (optional)

Position a rack in the center of the oven. Preheat the oven to 250°F/120°C. Line a rimmed baking sheet with parchment paper, and—this isn't necessary, but I find it helpful—use a pencil to trace around an 8-in/20-cm cake pan on the parchment paper. Flip the paper over, and set the baking sheet aside.

In a large, clean bowl using a handheld mixer or in the bowl of a stand mixer fitted with the whisk attachment, beat the egg whites on the lowest setting. After 15 seconds, gradually increase the speed to the highest setting. Once the mixture begins to foam, add the sugar and salt in a slow, steady stream.

The egg whites will begin to look glossy. Keep beating on high until firm (stiff) peaks form. The mixture should not feel granular when you rub it between your thumb and index finger, and the peak clinging on the wire whisk should stand with the utmost confidence.

Fold the vinegar into the meringue with a metal spoon to avoid deflating, then spoon the meringue onto the prepared baking sheet, spreading it out into the drawn circle (if you're freehanding it, try to keep it around 8 in/20 cm in diameter and 2 in/5 cm in height). Bake for 1 hour and 15 minutes, until the outside of the meringue has hardened and the center is still soft and chewy.

Allow the meringue to cool on its pan. Peel off the parchment and transfer the meringue to a plate or cake stand. Spoon on the whipped cream and top with the fruit of your choice and maybe a smattering of pistachio nuts before serving.

### note

The pavlova shell will keep, unfilled, in an airtight container at room temperature for up to 2 days. A filled pav is best eaten on the same day that you make it.

# STRAWBERRY NEW YORK CHEESECAKE

**MAKES ONE 9-IN/23-CM CAKE; SERVES 12 TO 16**

This recipe is dedicated to my late older cousin, Tito. He was one of the smartest, most encouraging people I knew. He taught me that communication is one of the most important things in life and that the panacea for all maladies is delicious food, especially a luscious cheesecake. When I was ten or eleven, we made one together—from his recipe, which I think was adapted from the recipe written on the inside of the cream cheese package. We sat the cheesecake in a water bath to cook; but unlike Tito, I'm a klutz and water baths are a messy business. I prefer this method: Put the uncooked cheesecake into a hot oven until it puffs up, then lower the temperature of the oven almost all the way; it works every time. This, to me, is the ultimate New York cheesecake; the cake stands tall with a strawberry topping, slightly crisp-crusted graham sides, and a soft, tender-crusted bottom. I think I've done Tito proud with this cheesecake.

## CRUST

**1½ cups/170 g graham cracker crumbs (see page 114 for homemade Graham Crackers)**

**6 Tbsp/85 g unsalted butter, melted**

**¼ cup/50 g granulated sugar**

**½ tsp pure vanilla extract**

**Pinch of fine-grain sea salt**

## FILLING

**2 lb/910 g cream cheese, at room temperature**

**1½ cups/300 g granulated sugar**

**2 Tbsp all-purpose flour**

**½ tsp finely grated lemon zest**

**½ tsp finely grated orange zest**

**3 large eggs plus 2 egg yolks, at room temperature**

**1 tsp pure vanilla extract**

**¾ cup/180 ml sour cream, at room temperature**

**½ cup/170 g Back of a Napkin Strawberry Jam (page 107)**

**TO MAKE THE CRUST:** Position a rack in the center of the oven. Preheat the oven to 450°F/230°C. Grease a 9-in/23-cm springform pan.

In a medium bowl, mix together the cracker crumbs, butter, sugar, vanilla, and salt. Press the mixture into the bottom and up the sides of the prepared pan, using your hands or the flat bottom of a small measuring cup to compress the crust. Put the pan in the freezer.

**TO MAKE THE FILLING:** In a large bowl using a handheld mixer (I find this works best for this job, rather than a stand mixer) beat the cream cheese, sugar, flour, lemon zest, and orange zest on medium speed for 3 to 5 minutes, stopping the mixer and scraping down the sides of the bowl and the beaters to make sure there's no lumpy cream cheese in sight.

With the mixer on its lowest speed, add the eggs, egg yolks, and vanilla all at once, mixing until smooth and the eggs are well incorporated. Mix in the sour cream until just incorporated.

*continued*

Remove the crust from the freezer, put the pan on a rimmed baking sheet, and wrap the sides of the pan with aluminum foil. Pour the filling into the prepared pan and put the pan on a baking sheet. Bake for 17 to 20 minutes, until the top is puffed. Lower the oven temperature to 225°F/110°C and bake until the cake is mostly firm but still slightly wobbly in the center, 45 minutes to 1 hour more. (If the cheesecake is not done after 45 minutes, check it every 5 minutes or so until it is—it seems like a daunting task, but cheesecake-making requires a bit of saintly patience.)

Once the cheesecake is done, remove it from the oven and allow it to cool to room temperature in the pan. Cover and refrigerate it for 8 hours before topping.

In a small saucepan over medium heat, combine the jam with 1 tsp water until it is pourable. Let it cool to room temperature and pour over the cheesecake. Return the cheesecake to the refrigerator until the jam topping is set before serving. The cheesecake will keep, covered, in the refrigerator for up to 5 days.

### note

You might not think there are enough graham cracker crumbs for the pan, but trust me, there are. Just work it into the pan using the flat bottom of a small measuring cup.

# spread a little butter on that!

She sets the large metal bowl in the old porcelain sink, pushes the faucet over it, and lets warm water dribble down her hand into the bowl. This is how my grandmother has always made bread. It's a casual act, yet one with confidence and gumption.

Bread making is definitely a good place to start as a novice baker. Although it will scare the living daylights out of you at first, it will teach you how dough feels during its different stages—and that is of the utmost importance. Bread making is about feeling and caring for a simple mix of ingredients, ones brought to life—most often—by yeast.

After baking your very first bread, you'll be impressed and childishly satisfied with yourself. It's quite an addictive activity.

One of the most important parts of bread making is kneading. It's required in almost all the recipes in this section. Most bread kneading, simply put, is the process of collecting dough into a single mass, warming and stretching it (more specifically, the gluten strands within it) with the heels of your hands onto itself many times until it's springy and smooth. Everyone has their own style of kneading, and if you're new to working with yeasted breads, you'll get a flow you stick with once you get into it.

The following recipes are of different degrees of difficulty, but are all quite easy to put together. What's most important is to simply follow the recipes and have faith, as everything will work out in your favor. I've offered advice and recommendations in the notes of each recipe.

One thing I repeat is the note about machine kneading, but I'll elaborate on it here, as it's quite important. If you're just starting to work with simple yeasted breads that require kneading, don't use any machinery for now. Getting a feel for the dough is essential before you move on to kneading dough in a stand mixer. Not only is kneading dough by hand a meditative act, it allows you to slow down in the middle of a bustling world, it lets you focus on your breath one fold at a time, and, most importantly, it gives you a moment to reflect on life and to feel how dough should be. After spending some time working with yeasted bread dough and learning how it should feel and look when it's kneaded, get out a stand mixer fitted with the dough hook attachment and knead away on the lowest setting until the dough is springy. Do make sure, however, that your mixer can handle kneading stiff doughs; refer to the manufacturer's instructions.

Please note that the quality of the flour used in your bread makes a huge difference in the final product. I like to use organic flours from some of the brands listed in the back of the book. These brands, of course, are not available in all countries, so use a brand that comes from a well-respected milling company where you live. Do keep in mind that all flours expire and go rancid eventually. If your flour begins to smell like wet paint, it needs replacing. Be sure that your flour is not past the expiration date marked on its package; this is of the utmost importance.

# NEW YORK–STYLE BAGELS

**MAKES 8 BAGELS**

**As a native New Yorker, I know there's nothing better for breakfast on the weekend than a fresh, toasted bagel schmeared with cream cheese. Now I live a state away, and I constantly crave the good old-fashioned bagels I grew up on—flavorful, modestly sweet, chewy ones with soft, shiny crusts. These bagels are made the classic way: You boil them for a couple of minutes in water before you bake them. This is probably one of the most bizarre things a person can do to dough, but it works. So, if good bagels can't be found where you live, worry no more; this recipe is infinitely adaptable, and the bit of effort you put into making these bagels is well worth it. Trust me on this. Use the photographs on page 182 as visual reference.**

**4½ tsp granulated sugar**

**1 tsp active dry yeast (see Note)**

**1½ cups/360 ml warm water (100°F to 110°F/38°C to 43°C)**

**4 cups/500 g bread flour or high-gluten flour, plus more as needed**

**1½ tsp fine-grain sea salt**

**Minced fresh garlic, minced fresh onion, poppy seeds, sesame seeds, caraway seeds, coarse salt, or cinnamon-sugar for topping (optional)**

**Cream cheese for serving**

Pour the sugar and yeast into ½ cup/120 ml of the warm water. Don't stir the mixture. After it sits for 5 minutes, there should be bubbles in the water; only then, stir the mixture until it all dissolves in the water.

In a large bowl, mix together the flour and salt using your hands. Make a well in the center of the flour, and pour in the yeast-sugar mixture.

Pour about ¾ cup/180 ml of the remaining warm water into the well. Using your hands, mix and stir in more warm water as needed *(1)*. Depending on the temperature, humidity, and type of flour you are using, you might need to add anywhere from 2 Tbsp to ¼ cup/60 ml water. You want the dough to be moist and firm after it's mixed.

Drop the dough onto a clean, lightly floured work surface and knead it for about 10 minutes, adding as much extra flour as you need to form a firm and stiff dough. Shape the dough into a round *(2)*.

Lightly oil a large bowl. Put the dough in the bowl and turn the dough to coat it all over. Cover the bowl with a clean, damp dish towel. Let the dough rise in a warm, draft-free place for about 2 hours, until the dough has doubled in size (if you decided to double the amount of yeast called for in the recipe, wait 1 hour). If you poke the dough with your finger and the impression remains, the dough is well risen; if it bounces back, it hasn't risen enough.

After the dough has had time to rise, punch down the dough and let it rest for another 10 minutes. Carefully divide the dough into eight equal portions (tip: if you're obsessive like me, use a scale for extra precision).

Hold your hand in a C shape and cup one dough portion. Press the dough against the work surface (avoid flouring it) while moving your hand and the dough in a slow circular motion, allowing the irregular edge of the dough to pull into itself, while decreasing the pressure on top of the dough slightly, until a perfectly smooth round ball forms; repeat with the seven other portions *(3)*. Have your eyes crossed? This probably does sound difficult at first, but essentially all you're doing is making the dough round taut by pulling its sides in and keeping it round.

Lightly oil a rimmed baking sheet. Coat a finger in flour and gently press your finger into the center of each dough ball to form a ring. Gently stretch the rings out (if you do this roughly, you'll likely end up with wrinkly, but still delicious bagels) to about a third of the diameter of the bagel *(4)*. Put them on the prepared baking sheet.

Cover the tray of dough with a slightly damp kitchen towel and allow it to rest for 10 minutes. Meanwhile, position a rack in the center of the oven. Preheat the oven to 425°F/220°C. Oil another baking sheet.

Bring a large pot of water to a bubbling boil and lower the heat. Use a slotted spoon or skimmer to place the bagels into the water. Poach as many bagels as can comfortably fit in the pot, allowing for some room, as they do puff up quite a bit. Once the bagels are in, they should float on the top. Let them sit there for 1 minute, and then flip them over to boil the other sides for 1 minute. Remove each bagel to a clean tea towel (avoid using a paper towel, as it will stick) or wire rack to drain.

If you'd like to top your bagels, do so now, sprinkling the garlic, onion, etc. over the bagels. Transfer the bagels to the second baking sheet. Bake for 20 minutes, until the bagels are uniformly golden brown.

Transfer the bagels to a wire rack to cool, or if you're impatient like I am, slice one of these babies open, and spread on some cream cheese. Take a bite . . . . Oooh, child! The bagels will keep in a resealable plastic bag at room temperature for up to 2 days.

## notes

Short on time? Increase the yeast called for in the recipe to 2 tsp to cut down on the time the dough takes to double in volume; this, however will lend a slightly more yeasty taste to your dough. So, if you don't have an extra hour to sacrifice, this is a good option that doesn't affect the quality of the bagels.

If you don't have access to bread flour, it's okay to use all-purpose flour; the bagels should still come out wonderfully. If you can find vital wheat gluten (it's usually carried at health food stores), add 4 tsp to your all-purpose flour, and you should have a good substitute for the bread flour called for in the recipe.

I like to make a double batch of this recipe (one plain and another with toppings) whenever I can. That way, I can enjoy bagels for a couple of weeks. I bake the bagels, let them cool completely, pre-slice them, and freeze them in freezer-safe bags. And whenever I want a bagel, I take it out of the freezer and put it in the toaster. Convenience at its best!

If you prefer, you can knead the dough in a stand mixer fitted with the paddle attachment, on the lowest setting, for 5 to 6 minutes, instead of kneading by hand. If you're making a double batch, you might not be able to use your stand mixer for kneading—refer to the manufacturer's instructions.

## variations

**CINNAMON-RAISIN BAGELS:** Under hot running water, wash 1½ cups/255 g raisins. Dry them to remove the natural yeast on the outside of the raisins. Sift together 1 Tbsp dark brown sugar or light muscovado sugar, ¼ cup/50 g granulated sugar, and 1 Tbsp ground cinnamon with the flour. Mix in the raisins, and proceed to making the dough.

**WHOLE-WHEAT BAGELS:** Simply use half whole-wheat flour and half bread flour.

**WHOLE-WHEAT AND SPELT BAGELS:** Use 2 cups/255 g whole-wheat flour and 2½ cups/315 g sifted spelt flour.

**BLUEBERRY/RASPBERRY BAGELS:** Mix 1½ cups/185 g, or per your taste, frozen berries (unthawed) into the dough.

2
3
4

# EASY-PEASY BRIOCHE

**MAKES ONE 8-PIECE PULL-APART LOAF**

**Brioche, like challah (see page 189), is egg and butter rich. It's perfect to serve at Sunday brunch with jars of Back of a Napkin jam (see page 107) and room-temperature butter. They're incredible served warm and, once they're stale, they're lovely to use for French toast or bread pudding.**

**1¾ cups/210 g all-purpose flour**
**1½ tsp granulated sugar**
**1¼ tsp quick-rise (instant) yeast**
**½ tsp fine-grain sea salt**
**6 Tbsp/85 g cold unsalted butter, cut into ½-in/12-mm cubes**
**2 Tbsp warm milk**
**3 large eggs, cold**

Lightly oil a large mixing bowl and set aside.

In the bowl of a food processor, combine the flour, sugar, yeast, and salt. Pulse in the butter until the mixture resembles coarse crumbs. Pulse in the milk and two of the eggs until mixed through. Leave the dough covered and allow it to rise directly in the food processor for 1 hour, until doubled in size.

Meanwhile, butter an 8-by-4-in/20-by-10-cm loaf pan and set aside.

Once the dough has doubled, press the pulse button once to deflate it. Carefully scoop the dough out onto a work surface (no need for extra flour here) and divide it into eight equal portions.

Hold your hand in a C shape and cup one dough portion. Press the dough against the work surface (avoid flouring it) while moving your hand and the dough in a slow circular motion, allowing the irregular edge of the dough to pull into itself, while decreasing the pressure on top of the dough slightly, until a perfectly smooth round ball forms; put it into the prepared loaf pan and repeat with the seven other portions.

Cover with buttered plastic wrap and let the dough rise in a warm, draft-free area for 1 hour, until doubled in size and the rounds are peeking out from the pan.

Forty-five minutes into the rise, position a rack in the center of the oven. Preheat the oven to 375°F/190°C.

Whisk the remaining egg with 1 tsp water and gently brush a light coating on the dough. Allow the egg glaze to dry for 1 minute.

Bake for 16 to 21 minutes (rotate the pan halfway through baking), until the bread is beautifully golden brown and a cake tester inserted into the loaf comes out clean. Cool slightly on a wire rack before serving. The loaf will keep in a resealable plastic bag at room temperature for up to 2 days.

# DOMINICAN WATER BREAD (PAN DE AGUA)

**MAKES 8 ROLLS**

**My fondest memory of this bread is from one of the many warm summers I spent in the Dominican Republic. The small bodega that sold these rolls was about half a block from my grandparents' home in the capital; the store also doubled as a bakery. I only set foot in the store once, with my grandfather, to buy the morning newspaper and candy bars. After my grandfather passed, my grandmother would call for a delivery of milk and these rolls every day, and within minutes there'd be a knock at the door with a man holding up a bag of milk and warm, soft Dominican water bread. We always have them at home now. They are great for sandwiches, but are far better, warm out of the oven, dipped in thick hot chocolate, just as my mother and grandmother taught me to do.**

**4 cups/500 g bread flour, plus more if needed**

**2 tsp fine-grain sea salt**

**1 tsp quick-rise (instant) yeast**

**1 tsp granulated sugar**

Lightly oil a rimmed baking sheet and set aside.

In a large bowl using a wooden spoon or in the bowl of a stand mixer fitted with the dough hook, mix together the flour, salt, yeast, and sugar. Mix in 2 cups/480 ml warm water (at low speed if you're using a mixer). The resulting dough will be quite wet and shaggy.

***If you're working by hand:***

Flour a clean, sturdy work surface and have a dough scraper nearby to help release any sticky dough as necessary. Knead the soft dough for 10 minutes, until it's smooth and elastic, dusting the surface with flour as needed. The dough will still be quite soft and tacky, but it won't stick to the surface as it did earlier.

***If you're working with the stand mixer:***

Simply run the mixer on low speed for 6 minutes, until the dough is smooth and elastic, adding more flour 1 Tbsp at a time if it sticks to the side of the bowl.

Allow the dough to rest for 10 minutes, then divide it into eight equal portions.

Hold your hand in a C shape and cup one dough portion. Press the dough against the work surface (avoid flouring it) while moving your hand and the dough in a slow circular motion, allowing the irregular edge of the dough to pull into itself, while decreasing the pressure on top of the dough slightly, until a perfectly smooth round ball forms; put it onto the prepared baking sheet and repeat with the seven other portions.

Cover with a clean, damp kitchen towel and let the dough rise in a warm, draft-free area for about 2 hours, until doubled in size.

continued

During the last 20 minutes of rising, position racks in the center and lower third of the oven. Preheat the oven to 475°F/240°C. Put a metal pan filled three-quarters full with warm water on the lowest rack in the oven. (Don't use nonstick or Teflon—it might be unable to withstand the intense heat of the oven. I use a large aluminum loaf pan.) Put the baking sheet on the middle rack in the oven and close the oven door immediately.

Bake for 15 minutes, then carefully remove the pan of hot water and let the rolls bake for 5 to 10 minutes more, until they are a beautiful golden brown.

Allow the rolls to cool for 15 minutes on the baking sheet before serving them warm. The rolls are best eaten the same day; however, they will keep in resealable plastic bags at room temperature for 1 day.

## note

Have faith: The dough for pan de agua is a little unusual compared to many doughs, as it is so soft because of the water-to-flour ratio. The dough should be as soft as chewing gum, so don't feel as if you're doing something wrong while making these rolls, especially if you're used to handling regular bread dough. Just have faith, as it will all work out in the end.

# RAISIN CHALLAH

**MAKES 1 ROUND BRAIDED LOAF**

On my way to my grandmother's house, there's a bakery that makes shiny-crusted, soft, rich raisin challah bread. I always pick up a loaf for our Saturday breakfast together. It's early morning; my dad unfurls the white paper bag of challah and begins cutting and buttering slices of the soft, raisin-specked bread. My grandmother sits at the end of the small, tiled breakfast table, basking in the sweet silence of the morning. My aunt, Samee, stands by the stove, preparing her famous ginger and cardamom–infused milk tea to go with the bread. I stand at the corner of the stove next to Samee, taking in the sweet, spiced smells. We all sit and pick at the buttered bread. After a couple of slices, we press the bread in half and dunk it in the warm tea. It's something we learned to do as children over cups of warm tea and stories of my grandmother's childhood in India. The bread is easy to execute—make an eggy dough of olive oil and honey, let it rest, divide and braid, and push the ends together to form a beautiful round. Use the photographs on page 190 as visual reference.

- ¾ cup/180 ml warm water (100°F to 110°F/38°C to 43°C)
- 2¼ tsp active dry yeast
- 1 tsp granulated sugar
- 6 Tbsp/90 ml vegetable oil or olive oil
- ¼ cup/60 ml honey
- 4 large eggs, at room temperature
- 1½ tsp fine-grain sea salt or kosher salt
- 3½ cups/420 g all-purpose flour
- ¾ cup/130 g raisins, washed under hot running water and dried

In a large bowl, pour in the warm water and sprinkle the yeast and sugar over it. Don't stir the mixture. After it sits for 5 minutes, there should be bubbles in the water; only then, stir the mixture until all the yeast dissolves in the water.

Whisk the vegetable oil, honey, three of the eggs, and the salt into the yeast mixture until everything is well incorporated. Use a wooden spoon or your hands to stir in the flour and raisins.

Drop the dough onto a clean, lightly floured work surface and knead it for 10 minutes, until it's smooth and elastic. Shape the dough into a round.

Lightly oil a large bowl, put the dough inside it, and turn the dough to coat all over. Cover the bowl with a clean, damp kitchen towel or plastic wrap. Let the dough rise in a warm, draft-free area for about 1 hour, until it has doubled in size.

Meanwhile, line a large (at least 9 in/23 cm in diameter) cast-iron skillet or a rimmed baking sheet with parchment paper and set aside.

After an hour of rising, punch down the dough (1) and divide it into three equal portions. Roll out each portion into an 18-in-/46-cm-long rope (if your work surface is short, make it about 12 in/30 cm). Lay the dough pieces parallel to one another, pinch together the ends nearest you, and begin braiding the pieces (2). Form the braided dough into a circle and pinch its ends together to form a round (3).

*continued*

2
3
4

Transfer the dough to the parchment-lined skillet (4). Whisk the remaining egg with 1 tsp water and gently brush the egg glaze all over the challah. Allow the glaze to dry for a few minutes, then brush more glaze all over the loaf again. Allow the braided dough to rise, uncovered, for 1 hour in a warm place.

Forty-five minutes into the rise, position a rack in the center of the oven. Preheat the oven to 375°F/190°C.

Bake for 30 to 40 minutes, rotating the pan halfway through, until the challah is completely bronzed and sounds hollow when you tap it on the bottom. If the challah has browned quite significantly when you check on it halfway through baking, loosely tent it with foil. Let the challah cool in the skillet for 10 minutes before transferring it to a wire rack to cool completely, or eat it right away. The challah will keep in a resealable plastic bag at room temperature for up to 3 days.

## note

Though it's perfect for Rosh Hashanah, this bread is also great for weekend breakfasts. After it's gone a little stale (usually after a couple of days), leftover raisin challah bread makes for great French toast and/or a lazy bread pudding (in which warm, steamy milk and sugar is spooned over the stale bread). You can even use leftover Pumpkin Filling (see page 68) for pumpkin pie French toast.

## variation

Some like it raisiny: If you prefer more raisins in your bread, add up to ¼ cup/40 g more; use whatever raisins you have on hand.

If you want to make this special, put the raisins in a medium bowl and top them off with simmered apple juice. Allow the raisins to sit for about 5 minutes, until they're plump. Strain and gently tap them dry on a paper towel or a clean kitchen towel before adding to the dough.

You can, of course, leave the raisins out and make a plain challah topped with sesame seeds or poppy seeds (or a combination).

# ANGELIC BISCUITS

**MAKES ABOUT 12 BISCUITS**

**Chilled proper ingredients and a light touch are crucial to making perfect buttermilk biscuits. I prefer a soft-sided biscuit, so I place the biscuits close together on the baking sheet. If you prefer more crust on your biscuits, simply place each one well apart from the others. I am partial to square biscuits, mostly because I don't like waste and I lack the patience to cut out rounds of dough and carefully reroll the dough scraps back together, which can deny the biscuits the angelically light texture I prefer. If you use a biscuit cutter, please try to cut each biscuit as close to the others as possible. You can reroll the dough to make additional biscuits, but it won't have the same puff that the others do; avoid rerolling gathered dough more than once.**

**1¾ cups/210 g all-purpose flour (try to use unbleached; it'll make for lighter biscuits)**

**⅓ cup/40 g cake flour or White Lily flour (see Note)**

**4 tsp aluminum-free baking powder (see page 15)**

**2 tsp granulated sugar**

**½ tsp fine-grain sea salt**

**½ cup/115 g cold unsalted butter (or shortening, lard, or duck fat; see Notes), cut into 16 pieces**

**⅔ cup/150 ml buttermilk, plus more for brushing**

Position a rack in the center of the oven. Preheat the oven to 400°F/205°C. Line a baking sheet with parchment or a silicone baking mat.

In a large bowl, whisk together the all-purpose flour, cake flour, baking powder, sugar, and salt. Using your fingertips or a pastry cutter, quickly cut and rub the butter into the flour mixture until it resembles pea-size pieces. It's okay if the pieces are not uniform; that is what you want.

Pour in the buttermilk. Using a fork, mix everything until it just comes together (it'll look like a shaggy mess). Turn the dough out onto a lightly floured work surface, lightly dust the top with flour, and gently knead the mass until it holds together.

With a rolling pin or your hands, quickly flatten the dough into a rectangle. Fold the short ends over the middle (like a letter) to make three layers. This is the first turn. Give the dough a quarter rotation and flatten it into a rectangle, then repeat the folding process. Repeat the flattening and folding once more.

Shape the dough into a rectangle ½ in/12 mm thick. If you want to stick with tradition, and keep the biscuits from puffing up into lopsided messes, use the tines of a fork to prick the dough. This is entirely optional.

Cut out the biscuits using a 2- to 2½-in/5- to 6-cm biscuit cutter (being careful not to twist the cutter as you work) or use a sharp knife to cut the biscuits into squares.

Gently move each biscuit to the prepared baking sheet. Set them about 1 in/2.5 cm apart for biscuits with a crust, or about ½ in/12 mm apart for soft-sided biscuits. Lightly brush the tops of each biscuit with a little buttermilk.

continued

Bake for 10 to 15 minutes, until the biscuits are tall and puffed and are blushing with a light golden-brown color around the edges. If you are making smaller biscuits, check on them after 9 minutes.

These are best if eaten immediately. However, if you must eat them at a later time, cool the biscuits on a wire rack once they're out of the oven. The biscuits will keep in large resealable plastic bags at room temperature for up to 1 day; just be sure to heat them up (out of the bags, of course) on a parchment-lined cookie sheet in a 250°F/130°C oven for a few minutes until they are warm and back to life.

## notes

Biscuit dough freezes exceptionally well. After cutting the dough, simply put the rounds on a baking sheet and freeze them. Once they're frozen, put them in an airtight resealable bag. There is no need to defrost them when it's time to bake. Just take them from bag to oven (but add a couple extra minutes to the baking time).

Chilled ingredients make for superior biscuits because they make for unbelievably flaky and tender dough, so make sure all your ingredients are cold. Chill the bowl and all the ingredients in the freezer for a few minutes.

Flour substitutes: If you do not have cake flour or White Lily flour on hand, you can use 2 cups/ 255 g total bleached all-purpose flour or a combination of all-purpose flour and whole-wheat pastry flour. If you want to use only White Lily flour, simply use 2¼ cups/290 g in place of the all-purpose flour and cake flour called for in the recipe.

Cold, unsalted butter is a necessity in my world. It's delicious and adds a lot of flavor to biscuits. Some argue that salted butter is better; however, it contains slightly less fat than unsalted butter, which means that it contains more water, which equals less flavor and less tender biscuits. Salted butter may not always be as fresh, either—the salt acts as a preservative. And, finally, I prefer to control the salt content of anything I bake; most bakers do. If salted butter is all you have on hand, do use it, keeping in mind that you have to cut back on salt used in the recipe.

Unsalted butter is not your only choice. Many people prefer shortening or lard (personally, I fear the stuff) in their biscuits because they produce very tender, flaky biscuits—it's all a matter of preference. If the shortening, lard, or duck-fat spirit moves you, please go for it; just make sure they're chilled!

A light touch is essential when making biscuits; don't handle the dough as you would bread dough. Touching and working your dough too much melts the butter and develops the gluten in the dough, making for undesirably tough biscuits. The less you touch the dough and the less you worry about uniformity, the better your biscuits will come out—I assure you!

# PENN STATION CINNAMON-SUGAR PRETZELS

**MAKES 12 PRETZELS**

**There are always interesting people walking around New York's Penn Station. These pretzels are the product of a visit to a vendor after I'd missed a train (it always happens to me) and had a run-in with an unusual character whose idea of a near-empty public waiting area was blurred with her idea of home, to say the least. The cinnamon-sugar pretzels I found myself buying after walking away from that uncomfortably comical event induced an "aha!" moment. These remind me of the kind of sweet cinnamon-sugar-covered pretzels you get at small pretzel shops in midtown Manhattan. They're beautifully bronzed, soft-centered yet chewy, and drizzled in sweet coffee glaze.**

## DOUGH

**1 cup/240 ml warm water (100°F to 110°F/38°C to 43°C)**

**2¼ tsp active dry yeast**

**2 tsp granulated sugar, plus 1½ Tbsp**

**¼ tsp fine-grain sea salt**

**2 cups/240 g all-purpose flour**

**1 cup/125 g bread flour**

**2 Tbsp unsalted butter, at room temperature**

**¼ cup/55 g baking soda**

## CINNAMON-SUGAR TOPPING

**¼ cup/50 g granulated sugar**

**2 tsp ground cinnamon**

**Pinch of fine-grain sea salt**

**¼ cup/55 g unsalted butter, melted**

**Coffee Glaze (recipe follows)**

**TO MAKE THE DOUGH:** In a small bowl, mix the water, yeast, 2 tsp sugar, and salt. Whisk until the sugar dissolves. Let stand until foamy, about 10 minutes.

In a large bowl, put in both flours and the butter. Using two butter knives, a pastry cutter, or your fingertips, cut the butter into the flour until the mixture resembles coarse crumbs.

Slowly pour the yeast mixture over the flour mixture, using a wooden spoon or your hands to combine. With your hands, gather the dough together. Turn the dough onto a lightly floured work surface and knead until it is no longer sticky, about 5 minutes.

Lightly oil a large bowl. Put the dough in the bowl and turn the dough to coat it all over. Cover the bowl with plastic wrap. Let the dough rise in a warm draft-free place for about 1 hour, until the dough has doubled in size.

Lightly oil a baking sheet. Cut the dough into twelve equal portions and roll each into an 18-in/46-cm rope. Form a U shape with each rope, and twist its ends together twice. Fold the twisted portions backward along the center of the U shape to form pretzel shapes, then gently press the ends of the rope onto the dough to seal. Transfer the pretzels to the baking sheet. Let them rise, uncovered, for 20 minutes.

Position a rack in the center of the oven. Preheat the oven to 475°F/240°C. Meanwhile, bring a large pot of water to a boil and add the baking soda and remaining 1½ Tbsp sugar. Lower the heat and boil the pretzel-shaped dough in batches (allowing some room for expansion) for 30 seconds per side, until puffed and slightly shiny. Transfer them to wire racks to drain. Return the pretzels to the prepared baking sheet.

Bake until golden brown and cooked through, about 15 minutes.

**TO MAKE THE TOPPING:** Mix together the sugar, cinnamon, and salt in a bowl; set aside.

Brush the melted butter on the tops of the pretzels immediately after you take them out of the oven. Sprinkle on some of the cinnamon-sugar, drizzle on the glaze, and serve immediately. The pretzels will keep, uncovered, at room temperature for up to 12 hours if you don't add the toppings. When you're ready to serve them, just warm them in a 250°F/130°C oven and add the topping and glaze.

### notes

These are also perfect warm and dipped in Tangy Cream Cheese frosting (page 28, sans orange juice and orange zest) instead of the Coffee Glaze. If you prefer plain pretzels, top them with coarse-grain sea salt once you've boiled them, then bake and serve them with your favorite mustard.

For some texture, top the pretzels off with your favorite combination of toasted chopped nuts after you've drizzled on the glaze.

# COFFEE GLAZE

**MAKES ¼ CUP/60 ML**

**This is a simple glaze with great flavor. It comes together quickly and can be used on anything from pretzels to Curiously Chewy Oatmeal Raisin Cookies (page 94).**

**2 tsp milk**

**2 tsp strong coffee**

**⅔ cup/65 g confectioners' sugar**

In a small bowl, whisk together the milk and coffee. Slowly stir in the confectioners' sugar, whisking until there are no longer any lumps. Use as needed.

### variations

If you prefer a glaze that isn't so intense, substitute half of the coffee with more milk.

If you want a glaze that is coffee-free, simply use all milk.

If you prefer to use vanilla instead of coffee, simply replace the coffee with 1 tsp pure vanilla extract and add another 1 tsp milk.

# resources

**INDIA TREE**
5309 Shilshole Ave NW, Suite 150
Seattle, WA 98107
800-369-4848
www.indiatree.com
Spices and muscovado sugar.

**KING ARTHUR FLOUR**
135 U.S. Route 5 South
Norwich, VT 05055
800-827-6836
www.kingarthurflour.com
Flours, kitchen tools, and equipment.

**NIELSEN-MASSEY**
1550 Shields Drive
Waukegan, IL 60085
800-525-7873
www.nielsenmassey.com
Vanilla extract, vanilla bean paste, and vanilla sugar.

**SCHARFFEN BERGER**
1192 Illinois Street
San Francisco, CA 94107
866-972-6879
www.scharffenberger.com
Chocolate and natural unsweetened cocoa powder.

**VALRHONA**
45 Main Street
Brooklyn, NY 11201
888-682-5746
www.valrhona-chocolate.com
Chocolate and unsweetened Dutch-processed cocoa powder.

**WILLIAMS-SONOMA**
3250 Van Ness Avenue
San Francisco, CA 94109
877-812-6235
www.williams-sonoma.com
Bakeware, cake decorating tools, marble boards, kitchen appliances, baking utensils, and books.

# acknowledgments

There are many people to thank for their help in the making of this book. Their words of encouragement and inspiration and their constant support are what pushed me to make this book what it is: the product of a small community.

I'd first like to thank my family. To my mother, whose hockey puck–like chocolate chip cookies inspired me to start baking all those years ago; thanks, Mom! To my sister, Sabrina, for always taste-testing my recipes and providing me with the most useful and honest feedback. To my Aunt Eunice and Uncle Paul, for constantly encouraging me to do my very best. To my late cousin Tito, who taught me that being adventurous in the kitchen is of the greatest importance. To my grandmothers, who have always cooked well and always cooked from scratch—thank you for inspiring me to keep that important tradition going. To my father—though we don't always agree on everything—whose endless kitchen experiments remind me that rules are sometimes meant to be broken. To my younger cousin who's like my little brother, Ahmer, who was diagnosed with stage-4 cancer and successfully fought it during the making of this book. To my Aunt Shahida, one of the best home cooks and strongest women I know. To my Aunt Samee, a fellow lover of chocolate and baked goods; thank you for introducing me to vanilla wafers as a child! And to the rest of my family, for always supporting my crazy ideas.

To my eighth-grade English teacher, Ms. Rygalski, and my high school teacher, coach, and friend Gail Bauwens; if you're reading this, thank you for changing my view of writing and teaching me how to find my voice, how powerful words can be, and how greatly they can impact a person's life. Thank you for being so passionate about your crafts.

I'd also like to thank my best friends, Sarah and Mikayla, for their constant support throughout the making of this book. Your words of encouragement, your honesty, and your jokes made the entire process easier, even when I thought it would be impossible.

There's also Lauren McMillan, a friend I made through food blogging. Thank you for constantly lending me an ear and for inspiring me with your thoughtful words when I needed them the most!

To all my other friends and acquaintances who willingly sampled my recipes and always swooned over them—thank you for making me smile and for offering me your ideas.

To Lorena Jones, for searching the Internet for doughnuts, finding my blog, and changing this guy's entire life—thank you for believing in me.

To Amy Treadwell, my amazing editor, who managed this project and helped to make my words clearer—thank you for everything.

To Alice Chau for doing such an amazing job on the design of this book.

To the rest of the amazing Chronicle team, David Hawk, Doug Ogan, Marie Oishi, Peter Perez, and Steve Kim.

To Shauna James Ahern, for constantly inspiring me to be real, to write from the heart, and for introducing me to my amazing agent, Stacey Glick of Dystel & Goderich. And to the remarkable Stacey, thank you for being a rock star, lending me your ear, offering me advice when I needed it, and for always loving my baked goods!

To Rachael White, my very first foodie friend; we've yet to meet in person, but I can't thank you enough for welcoming me with open arms into the online food-writing community. If you hadn't done so, I don't think I'd be here today—writing about food and sharing my recipes and life with others in a book.

To the readers and followers of The Sophisticated Gourmet; thank you for everything—for rooting me on and for supporting me in all that I've done throughout the years!

To you, my dear reader; though these thanks may seem clichéd, I am so grateful to you for bringing this book into your kitchen and for trusting me to guide you with delicious, reliable recipes. Thank you!

# index

## C